ILLUSTRATOR 7 — KEYBOARD SHORTCUTS

Note: The following is a list for the Macintosh. Windows users can use this list but should substitute Control for Command and Alt for Option.

VIEWING

Command-Y	Preview/Artwork Mode
F	Toggle Through Screen Viewing Modes
Command-R	Show/Hide Rulers
Command-Control-U	Cycle Through Measurement Systems
Command-Slash	Online Help
Command-Quote (")	Show/Hide Grid
Command-Shift-Quote (")	Toggle Snap to Grid
Command-Semicolon (;)	Show/Hide Guides
Command-Option-Semicolon (;)	Lock/Unlock Guides
Command-H	Hide/Show Edges
Command-Plus Sign (+)	Zoom In
Command-Minus Sign (-)	Zoom Out
Command-0	Fit in window
Command-1	Actual Size
Command-5	Make Guides
Command-Option-5	Release Guides

TYPE

Option-Right Arrow	Open Kerning
Option-Left Arrow	Close Kerning
Option-Command-Right Arrow	Open Kerning in increments of 5
Option-Command-Left Arrow	Close Kerning in increments of 5
Option-Up Arrow	Close Leading
Option-Down Arrow	Open Leading
Command-Shift-L	Align Flush Left
Command-Shift-R	Align Flush Right
Command-Shift-C	Align Center
Command-Shift-Less Than (<)	Down in Point Size
Command-Shift-Greater Than (>)	Up in Point Size
Option-Shift-Up Arrow	Baseline Shift Up
Option-Shift-Down Arrow	Baseline Shift Down
Option-Shift-Command-Up Arrow	Baseline Shift Up in increments of 5
Option-Shift-Command-Down Arrow	Baseline Shift Down in increments of 5
Command-Shift-J	Justifies Area Text
Command-Shift-F	Force Justified Area Text
Command-Shift-X	Resets Horizontal Scale to 100%
Command-Shift-Q	Resets Tracking to 0

SELECTING

Command-L	Lock All
Command-Shift-L	Unlock All
Command-U	Hide Selection
Command-Shift-U	Show Selection
Command-Tab	Toggle Between Selection and Direct Selection Tools
Command-A	Select All
Command-Shift-A	Deselect All
Command-G	Group
Command-Shift-G	Ungroup

TRANSFORMATIONS

Command-D	Repeat Transform
Command-Tilde (~)	Puts Focus in Selected Palette
Tilde (~)	When used with Polygon Tools, creates duplicates; when used with transformation tools, transforms only pattern fills

FUNCTIONS

Command-J	Join
Command-Option-J	Average
Command-Z	Undo
Command-Shift	Redo
Command-X	Cut
Command-C	Copy
Command-V	Paste
F-12	Revert
Command-4	Repeat Pathfinder
Command-F	Paste in Front
Command-B	Paste in Back
Command-Open Bracket	Send Backwards
Command-Shift-Open Bracket	Send to Back
Command-Closed Bracket	Bring Frontwards
Command-Shift-Closed Bracket	Bring to Front
Command-7	Make Mask
Command-Option-7	Release Mask
Command-8	Make Compound Path
Command-Option-8	Release Compound Path
Command-Shift-O	Convert text to outlines
Command-E	Apply Last Filter
Command-Option-E	Last Filter (brings up dialog box)

PALETTES

Command-I	Toggles Color Palette
Tab	Hides All Palettes
Shift-Tab	Hides All Palettes Except Tool Bar
Command-T	Toggles Character Palette
Command-M	Toggles Paragraph Palette
F-5	Toggles Swatches Palette
F-6	Toggles Color Palette
F-7	Toggles Layers Palette
F-8	Toggles Info Palette
F-9	Toggles Gradient Palette
F-10	Toggles Stroke Palette
F-11	Toggles Attributes Palette
Command-Shift-I	Toggles Attributes Palette

SHORTCUTS

Control (Macintosh)	Activates Context-sensitive pop-up menu
Right Mouse Button (Windows)	Activates Context-sensitive pop-up menu
Command-Option	Toggles the Convert Direction Point Tool
Command	Toggles the Last Used Selection Tool
Spacebar	Toggles the Hand Tool
Command-Spacebar	Toggles Zoom Tool
Command-Option-Spacebar	Toggles Zoom Out Tool
Comma (,)	Color
Period (.)	Gradient
Slash (/)	None Attribute
X	Toggles between Fill and Stroke
D	Sets fill and stroke to default (White Fill, Black Stroke)

TOOLS

V	Selection Tool
A	Direct Selection/Group Selection Tool
P	Pen Tool/Add Anchor Point Tool/Delete Anchor Point Tool/Convert Direction Point Tool
T	Type Tool/Area Type Tool/Path Type Tool/Vertical Type Tool/Vertical Area Type Tool/Vertical Path Type Tool
N	Ellipse Tool/Centered Ellipse Tool/Polygon Tool/Star Tool/Spiral Tool
M	Rectangle Tool/Rounded Rectangle Tool/Centered Rectangle Tool/Centered Rounded Rectangle Tool/Pencil Tool/Paintbrush Tool
C	Scissors Tool/Knife Tool
R	Rotate Tool/Twirl Tool
S	Scale Tool/Reshape Tool
O	Reflect Tool
W	Shear Tool
B	Blend Tool/Auto Trace Tool
J	All Graph Tools
U	Measurement Tool
G	Gradient Tool
K	Paint Bucket Tool
I	Eyedropper Tool
H	Hand Tool/Page Tool
Z	Zoom Tool

Teach
Yourself
ILLUSTRATOR 7
in 24 Hours

Teach Yourself

ILLUSTRATOR 7
in 24 Hours

Mordy Golding

Hayden
Books

201 West 103rd Street
Indianapolis, Indiana 46290

Teach Yourself Illustrator 7 in 24 Hours
©1997 Hayden Books

Library of Congress Catalog Number: 97-72170
ISBN: 1-56830-410-2

Copyright © 1997 Hayden Books

Printed in the United States of America 1 2 3 4 5 6 7 8 9 0

Warning and Disclaimer

Trademark Acknowledgments

President   Richard K. Swadley
Publisher   John Pierce
Managing Editor   Lisa Wilson
Director of Marketing   Kelli S. Spencer
Product Marketing Manager   Kim Margolius

Acquisitions Editor
Rachel Byers

Development Editor
Beth Millett

Copy/Production Editor
Kevin Laseau

Technical Editors
Kate Binder

Publishing Coordinator
Karen Williams

Marketing Coordinator
Linda Beckwith

Cover Designer
Tim Amrhein

Book Designer
Gary Adair

Manufacturing Coordinator
Brook Farling

Production Team Supervisors
Brad Chinn
Andrew Stone

Production Team
Carol Bowers
Cyndi Davis-Hubler
Chris Livengood
Gene Redding
Janet Seib

Indexer
Johnna L. VanHoose

Contents at a Glance

Contents

Dedication

To my loving wife, Batsheva.

Acknowledgments

To Rachel, Beth, and all the great folks at Hayden Books for keeping the faith and for turning yet another dream into a reality.

To Ted and Jen Alspach for their warm friendship and never-ending advice. It's the little things in life—right, guys?

To Sandee Cohen for taking me by the hand and bringing me into the fold. For all those hours on the phone, and for a friend who doesn't know how to say no.

To Sharon Steuer for constantly reminding me to spend more time with my family. If only I had listened to her more.

To all my "Illustrator Buddies" on AOL. There are too many to mention, but you all know who you are :)

To the 7:58 "train gang": Danny, Stuie, Michael, and the Daf for keeping me sane.

To Yisroel Golding, who started it all when in a cramped little room in St. Louis, he showed me Adobe Illustrator 88 on something called Macintosh. I still remember the day clearly…

To my parents, who always knew that I *could* do it, but just never thought that I actually *would*.

To the Wrotslavsky family for *still* believing in me.

Most of all, to my dearest wife Batsheva, my daughter Chayala, and my son Simcha, whose support, love, and most importantly, smiles keep me going every day of my life.

About the Authors

Mordy Golding

A trainer, consultant, writer, graphic designer, production artist, network manager, husband, and a father (not necessarily in that order), Mordy resides in Long Island, NY where he spends too much time sitting in front of a computer, fiddling with his web site (`http://www.mordy.com`), and not enough time with his loving family. With a strong technical background, Mordy has been designing on computers since 1990, and is a featured panelist at Macworld. Mordy also loves replying to email (mordy@mordy.com).

Hayden Books

The staff of Hayden Books is committed to bringing you the best computer books. What our readers think of Hayden is important to our ability to serve our customers. If you have any comments, no matter how great or how small, we'd appreciate your taking the time to send us a note.

You can reach Hayden Books at the following:

Hayden Books
201 West 103rd Street
Indianapolis, IN 46290
317-581-3833
Internet: hayden@hayden.com

Visit the Hayden Books web site at http://www.hayden.com

Introduction

"Teach yourself Illustrator in 24 hours?" Yeah, right. I'll bet you're thinking you could probably learn how to do a triple-bypass open heart procedure before you could learn Adobe Illustrator (those guys on E.R. make it look so easy). But it can be done, and this book is the perfect way to learn how. I've broken down the entire application into easy-to-understand chapters, and before you know it, you'll be a proficient Illustrator user. Trust me, it's *a lot* simpler than medical school...

Who Should Read This Book

If you've already picked up the book and started reading, you're probably interested in learning Illustrator, and—Behold! This book was written for anyone who wants to learn Illustrator! Whether you're an experienced Photoshop user who wants to enjoy the precise illustration benefits of Illustrator, a FreeHand convert, an experienced Illustrator user who wants to get up to speed with the new version 7, or a beginner, this book is a great way to quickly learn Illustrator.

Can This Book Really Teach Illustrator in 24 Hours?

I think the comic Steven Wright said it best: A guy walks down to a 24 hour convenience store at 2:00 a.m. to see the owner locking up the store. The guy incredulously says, "But it says you're open 24 hours!" The owner replies, "Yeah, but not in a row."

You do yourself a tremendous disservice if you try to read this entire book in one day (to say nothing of the disservice you'd be doing to your social life). It is impossible to learn a complex illustration program in one sitting. By spending a few solid hours at comfortable intervals, however, *you can*.

This book has been carefully organized so that you can systematically progress, learning more and more about Illustrator—whether you do it in a few days, weeks, or even months. As with the great sage who observed the little drops of water that eventually bored through the rock, each hour you spend in Illustrator brings you that much closer to mastering the program.

What This Book Assumes

This book was written on the assumption that you are already familiar with certain concepts, ideas, and techniques.

I will take it for granted that you already know how to use your computer—turning it on and off, launching applications, choosing printers, and other basic computer functions. You should also already be familiar with using the mouse (if you just dropped the book, let out a shriek, and ran, this book is not for you).

Typographical Conventions

- The first time a new term appears, it is italicized.
- Accessing commands on menus or submenus is shown with the name of the menu, an arrow, then the command or submenu. For example: "Choose File➡Open" means choose Open from the File menu.
- Macintosh keyboard shortcuts appear in parentheses, and Windows keyboard shortcuts appear in brackets, like this (Command-A)[Command-A].

Terminology

Throughout the book, I may ask you to perform certain functions, which I will list below to avoid any confusion.

- **Click**—Press the mouse button and release it quickly.
- **Double-click**—Press the mouse button twice in rapid succession and release it.
- **Drag**—Simply move the mouse.
- **Press and drag**—Press the mouse button, and without releasing it, drag the mouse. Release the button only when instructed.

Now, let's learn a little more about what Illustrator is, and how it works.

Hour 1

Getting to Know Illustrator

With the release of Illustrator 7, Adobe has completed a tightly integrated trio of applications (Photoshop 4, PageMaker 6.5, and now Illustrator) that all work in the same way. Most key commands are the same across all applications, and palettes look and work the same. The applications are truly cross-platform, working virtually identically on both the Macintosh and Windows 95/Windows NT platforms. If you are already familiar with Photoshop, many things will be familiar to you as you learn Illustrator.

If you are already an Illustrator user, you will need to adjust to version 7's new interface, and its metaphors. And for those new to Illustrator in general, this chapter will deal with how Illustrator works, and how it differs from other graphics programs.

This hour, we will learn about:

- ☐ Raster and vector images
- ☐ Illustrator's environment
- ☐ Illustrator's tools and palettes
- ☐ Views in Illustrator

JUST A MINUTE

> Illustrator 7 is a major program upgrade. Whereas the last Macintosh version was 6, the last Windows version of Illustrator was 4.1. Version 7 finally brings identical features to both platforms while sporting a completely revised user interface. If you've used Illustrator before, you may go through a short transitional phase to get used to working in version 7.

Raster vs. Vector

In the ever-growing world of computer graphics, there are two types of images — raster and vector. Some programs that create *raster* images (also known as pixel or paint images) are Photoshop, MacPaint, PC Paintbrush, or Painter. Some programs that create *vector* art (also known as object-oriented art) are Illustrator (that's us!), FreeHand, MacDraw, and Expression. Other programs, such as Canvas and CorelDRAW, have tools to create both raster and vector images.

Raster Images

Raster images are made up of a whole lot of tiny dots, called *pixels*. To illustrate this concept, we will use a sheet of graph paper. Each square on the sheet represents one pixel (see Figure 1.1). Let's start simple and create a black and white circle that is 20 pixels in diameter (see Figure 1.2). The number of pixels determines the *resolution* of your file. The computer stores this file by recording the exact placement and color of each pixel (see Figure 1.3). The computer has no idea that it is a circle, only that it is a collection of little dots.

1

Figure 1.1.

Each square in the raster represents one pixel.

Figure 1.2.

A raster circle.

Figure 1.3.

Each pixel has a coordinate, and the contents of that pixel are recorded and saved in a file.

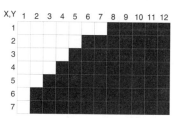

In this example, we saw each individual pixel, and the circle was very blocky. By adding more pixels, thereby increasing the resolution, we can make that same circle appear smoother because the pixels are much smaller (see Figure 1.4). Of course, the higher your resolution is, the larger your file size will be because the computer has many more pixels to keep track of.

Where the problem arises is when you try enlarging a raster image. Because the resolution is set, when you scale the art, in reality, you are just enlarging the pixels (see Figure 1.5), which results in a jaggy (or *pixelated*) image.

Figure 1.4.
By creating a circle with a higher resolution, we are able to make edges appear smoother at the cost of having a larger file size.

Figure 1.5.
At 100% (left), the circle appears to have a smooth edge. Enlarging the circle, however, reveals the jaggy edges (right).

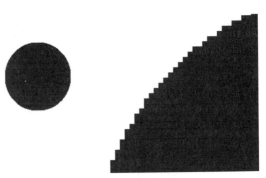

Vector Images: An Objective Approach

Vector art is different in that instead of creating individual pixels, you create objects, such as rectangles and circles. By noting the mathematical coordinates of these shapes, a vector program can store files in a fraction of the space as raster images, and more importantly, be able to scale images to virtually any size without any loss in detail (see Figure 1.6).

Figure 1.6.
Unlike raster images, the vector circle appears smooth at 100% (left) and just as smooth when enlarged 800% (right).

The Illustrator Workplace

Now that we know all about Illustrator, let's actually open it up and see what it has to offer. If it isn't already installed, follow the instructions that came with Illustrator to install it on your computer. Now, let's launch Adobe Illustrator 7.

JUST A MINUTE

If you've launched Illustrator before, or if you're working on someone else's computer, it's a good idea to trash your Preferences file so that what you see pictured in this book matches what you see onscreen. Follow these steps to trash your files.

On a Macintosh:

1. In the Finder, open your System Folder.
2. In your System Folder is a folder called Preferences. Open it.
3. Find and select the file in your Preferences folder called *Adobe Illustrator 7 Prefs*.
4. Drag it to the Trash, and empty the Trash.

On Windows:

1. Locate the Illustrator application folder.
2. Within the Illustrator application folder is a folder called Preferences. Open it.
3. Find and select the *Illustrator Preferences File*.
4. Drag it to the Recycle Bin and empty the Recycle Bin.

The next time you launch Illustrator, a sparkling new Preferences file is automatically created.

Did you know that you can edit Illustrator's Preferences file? If you're the daring type, open the file in a text editor and you can make changes, such as turning off warning dialog boxes.

CAUTION

You should learn how to trash your Preferences file, as it is a great troubleshooting tip. If Illustrator seems to be acting weird, or even crashing often, trashing the preferences and restarting Illustrator usually clears things up.

After viewing the beautiful Illustrator splash screen and trying to read all the names of the programmers to see whether you know any of them, you are presented with Illustrator's working environment and an open Untitled document—we're ready for action.

The Illustrator Window

First, let's take a tour of the Illustrator window. We'll start with a general look at Illustrator (see Figure 1.7) and then go into more detail about each part.

Figure 1.7.

Welcome to Illustrator. This is what Illustrator looks like when you open it for the first time.

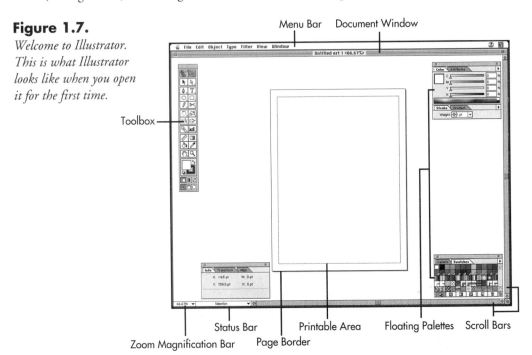

Across the top of the screen is the menu bar, which contains Illustrator's commands and essentials such as printing, saving, copying, and pasting.

Directly underneath is the document window, which is the actual Illustrator file. In the title bar of the document window is the filename and the percentage at which it is currently being viewed.

On the far left of the screen is a tall narrow strip of boxes. This is the Toolbox, which contains the tools you will use to work in Illustrator.

In the center of your screen you will see the page border of your document. You can change the page size to fit whatever you might need—anywhere from 2×2 inches to 120×120 inches.

Right inside the page border is a dotted line that represents the physical print area of the printer. Illustrator determines this by taking information from the PPD (PostScript Printer Definition) file of your currently selected printer.

At the upper-right side of the screen you will find four of Illustrator's many floating palettes: Color, Attributes, Stroke, and Gradient. They are clustered and docked, which we will soon see when we discuss palettes in detail.

At the lower-right side of the screen you will find two more floating palettes: the Layers palette and the active Swatches palette.

At the very bottom of the document window, as well as along the right side, are scroll bars. By clicking the arrows at each end, or by dragging the box within the scroll bar, you can move your page around within the document window. Now that you've learned what it is, don't ever use it. We will learn far more efficient ways to move around as we progress.

To the left of the scroll bar at the bottom of the document window is the status bar. Clicking the mouse on the status bar allows you to choose to have Illustrator display important information for you as you work. Or try holding down the (Option)[Alt] key while pressing the mouse button on the status bar for a list of not-so-important things to keep track of.

Immediately to the left of the status bar is the zoom magnification bar, which identifies the current zoom percentage of your file. You can quickly zoom to any of Illustrator's zoom percentages by clicking the mouse button with the cursor on this bar and selecting a zoom percentage.

The Toolbox

How can you keep track of Illustrator's different tools (see Figure 1.8)? Well, I can give you a hint—look at your *cursor*. Sometimes it's an arrow, other times a crosshair, a paintbrush, or different variations of a pen (see Figure 1.9). By recognizing the different cursors, you will be able to concentrate more on what you're drawing rather then on how to draw it. Wherever appropriate, I will bring these tell-tale cursors to your attention.

Figure 1.8.

The Illustrator Toolbox.

Figure 1.9.

Depending on different circumstances, the Pen tool cursor changes to quickly help you complete your drawing.

I strongly suggest that you learn the keyboard shortcuts for the Toolbox. Adobe has made it easy by assigning single keystrokes to every tool (see Figure 1.10). For tools that have several options (such as the Rectangle tool), hit the shortcut key repeatedly to cycle through the tools.

Figure 1.10.

You're dragging the mouse over the Toolbox when a tool tip pops up, identifying the tool and the keyboard shortcut for it.

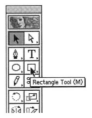

The following is a brief description of the tools found in the Illustrator Toolbox. The keyboard shortcut for each tool is in parentheses following the tool name.

You'll notice that a lot more tools are listed than what appear in the Illustrator Toolbox. To make life easier on all of us, tools that are similar in function are grouped together in the Toolbox. Those tools with a little black arrow in the lower-right corner of the box have other tools in their space. You can access these tools by either clicking and dragging the tool, which brings up a pop-up box of the tools in that group, or press the keyboard shortcut command for that tool repeatedly to cycle through all the tools in that space.

1

JUST A MINUTE

Do not be alarmed if you find a tool in the Toolbox that is not listed here. Illustrator 7 enables the addition of third-party plug-ins and the ability to place those plug-ins directly into the Illustrator Toolbox. VectorTools from Extensis, for instance, adds a Magic Wand selection tool to the Toolbox.

Selection Tools

Used most often, the selection tools are used to tell Illustrator which objects you are working on. The selection tools are

- ☐ **The Selection tool (V)**—Used to select and move objects.
- ☐ **The Direct Selection tool (A)**—Used to select parts of an object.
- ☐ **The Group Selection tool (A)**—A variation of the Direct Selection tool, used to select grouped items.

Creation Tools

It would be kind of silly if you couldn't create anything in Illustrator, right? The creation tools allow you to create your artwork, each tool serving a specific drawing task. The creation tools are

- ☐ **The Pen tool (P)**—Used to create Bézier paths.
- ☐ **The Add Anchor Point tool (P)**—Adds an anchor point to an existing path.
- ☐ **The Delete Anchor Point tool (P)**—Removes an existing anchor point.
- ☐ **The Convert Direction Point tool (P)**—Changes a selected anchor point of one type into another.
- ☐ **The Type tool (T)**—Used to create headline or point type.
- ☐ **The Area Type tool (T)**—Used to create area or paragraph type.
- ☐ **The Path Type tool (T)**—Used to create type on a path.
- ☐ **The Vertical Type tool (T)**—Used to create vertical headline or point type.
- ☐ **The Vertical Area Type tool (T)**—Used to create vertical area or paragraph type.
- ☐ **The Vertical Path Type tool (T)**—Used to create vertical text on a path.
- ☐ **The Ellipse tool (N)**—Creates circles and ovals.
- ☐ **The Centered Ellipse tool (N)**—Creates circles and ovals from a center origin point.
- ☐ **The Polygon tool (N)**—Creates polygons.
- ☐ **The Star tool (N)**—Creates multipointed stars.
- ☐ **The Spiral tool (N)**—Creates spirals.

- **The Rectangle tool (M)**—Creates squares and rectangles.
- **The Centered Rectangle tool (M)**—Creates squares and rectangles from a center origin point.
- **The Rounded Rectangle tool (M)**—Creates squares and rectangles with rounded corners.
- **The Centered Rounded Rectangle tool (M)**—Creates squares and rectangles with rounded corners from a center origin point.
- **The Pencil tool (Y)**—Used to draw freehand single path lines.
- **The Paintbrush tool (Y)**—Used to create filled variable-width objects, and supports pressure-sensitive tablets.
- **The Scissors tool (C)**—Splits a path at a selected point.
- **The Knife tool (C)**—Splits objects by slicing through them.

Transformation Tools

Power is being able to change that which you have. Illustrator's transformation tools give you the power you need to perfect your art. The transformation tools are

- **The Rotate tool (R)**—Used to rotate selected objects.
- **The Twirl tool (R)**—Used to distort selected objects in a circular fashion.
- **The Scale tool (S)**—Used to resize selected objects.
- **The Reshape tool (S)**—Used to make simple changes in the shape of a Bézier segment.
- **The Reflect tool (O)**—Used to mirror selected objects.
- **The Shear tool (W)**—Used to skew or slant selected objects.

Assorted Tools

Some tools just can't be categorized. Illustrator contains a wealth of task-specific tools to assist you in your quest for the perfect art. Illustrator's remaining tools are

- **The Blend tool (B)**—Creates blends between objects.
- **The Autotrace tool (B)**—Traces bitmapped art and converts it to vector.
- **The Graph tool (J)**—Creates an assortment of different graphs.
- **The Measure tool (U)**—Used to measure distance and angles.
- **The Gradient tool (G)**—Used to control the way gradients are filled within an object.
- **The Paint Bucket tool (K)**—Used to copy fill and stroke attributes from one object to another.

1

- ☐ **The Eyedropper tool (I)**—Used to sample fill and stroke attributes for use with the Paint Bucket tool.
- ☐ **The Hand tool (H)**—Used to "grab" the page and move it within the document window.
- ☐ **The Page tool (H)**—Used to position artwork on the printed page.
- ☐ **The Zoom tool (Z)**—Used to zoom both in and out of your document.

Underneath the tools are two swatches depicting the currently selected fill and stroke colors, with a small button on the lower left to quickly set the fill and stroke back to the default white fill, black stroke (D), and a small button on the upper right to swap the fill and stroke (see Figure 1.11). Using the X key toggles focus between fill and stroke. You'll learn more about these features in Hours 10 and 11, "Fills" and "Strokes."

Figure 1.11.

The fill and stroke selectors. If you use Photoshop, these are identical to the foreground and background swatches.

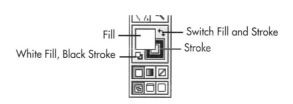

Below the fill and stroke selectors are three buttons (as shown in Figure 1.12) that you can use to quickly access Color (,), Gradient (.), and the None attribute (/).

Figure 1.12.

Quick-click shortcuts to the Color and Gradient palettes, as well as the None attribute.

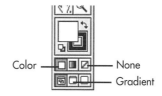

Finally, at the bottom of the Toolbox are three options for document viewing: standard screen mode, full screen mode with menu bar, and full screen mode (see Figure 1.13).

Figure 1.13.

Also similar to Photoshop are options to hide the menu bar and view a file full screen.

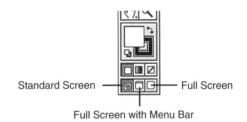

Standard Screen ———— Full Screen

Full Screen with Menu Bar

The Many Palettes of Illustrator

I think it all began when someone said, "Hey, the Toolbox is always visible, why can't we have other stuff also always visible?" Thanks to that one person, we now have *floating palettes*. They're called floating palettes because no matter what you are working on, they still remain in the foreground, accessible at all times. They can also be moved around by pressing and dragging the mouse over the title bar at the top of each palette.

The people at Adobe must really like floating palettes, because they gave Illustrator 13 of them (see Figure 1.14):

- [ ] Info palette
- [ ] Transform palette
- [ ] Align palette
- [ ] Color palette
- [ ] Gradient palette
- [ ] Stroke palette
- [ ] Swatches palette
- [ ] Layers palette
- [ ] Attributes palette
- [ ] Character palette
- [ ] Paragraph palette
- [ ] Multiple Master Design palette
- [ ] Tab palette

Throughout the book, we learn how to use each of these to our advantage.

1

Figure 1.14.

If you opened every Illustrator palette onscreen, you wouldn't have much room left to draw anything.

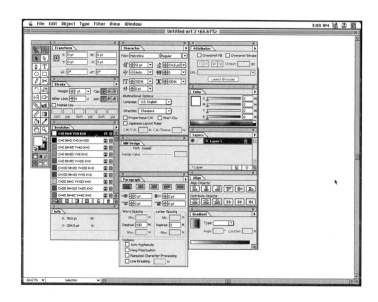

TIME SAVER

Screen real estate is really valuable, so it's nice that you can quickly hide all palettes at any time by hitting the Tab key. To hide all palettes except the Toolbox, press Shift-Tab.

Working with Palettes

Well, if you want to criticize Illustrator for having too many floating palettes, then you must also praise Illustrator for making it so easy to manage them. All of Illustrator's palettes "stick" to each other like magnets. They also stick to the edge of the screen window, which makes positioning them easy.

But it gets even better than that. Double-click the tab (the *tab* is the area where the actual name of the palette appears) of a floating palette, and the palette collapses, showing you only the tab (see Figure 1.15). Double-click the tab again to expand the palette.

Figure 1.15.

Double-clicking a tab collapses the palette.

You already know that you can position a floating palette by grabbing the top bar of the palette, but you get an extra surprise when you grab the tab of a palette. Clicking the tab of a palette and dragging produces the outline of the palette (see Figure 1.16). Now drag the outline right over the middle of another palette. Notice that the underlying palette now has a black outline around it (see Figure 1.17). Let go of the mouse button, and both palettes are now clustered (see Figure 1.18). Click the tab to bring that palette to the foreground. This capability gives you unlimited possibilities to configure your palettes.

Figure 1.16.

Dragging a palette by its tab.

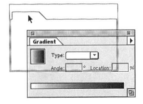

Figure 1.17.

Notice how the palette underneath becomes "selected" with a black outline.

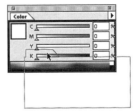

Figure 1.18.

The new clustered palette.

Believe it or not, there's even another way to configure palettes called *docking*. Grab the tab from a palette, and drag it over so that your mouse cursor just touches the bottom of another palette (see Figure 1.19). Notice there is a black outline only along the bottom of the underlying palette. When you release the mouse, the two palettes are docked (see Figure 1.20). You can now move the entire palette as one, but still collapse and cluster each palette individually. Cool, huh?

Figure 1.19.

Positioning a palette for docking.

1

Figure 1.20.
The palettes, docked.

Views in Illustrator

There are three *viewing modes* in Illustrator: Preview, Artwork, and Preview Selection. You can toggle between Preview and Artwork viewing modes by pressing (Command-Y) [Control-Y]. In Preview mode, you see the file as it would print, with colored fills and strokes (see Figure 1.21). There are times when it is necessary to view your file in Artwork mode where you see only the outline of each object (see Figure 1.22). Finally, the last view mode, Preview Selection (Command-Shift-Y)[Control-Shift-Y] is a combination of the two (see Figure 1.23). Whichever object you have selected shows in Preview mode, while all other artwork appears in Artwork mode. This is very useful when working on large files that seem to take years to redraw.

Figure 1.21.
A page viewed in Preview mode.

Figure 1.22.
A page viewed in Artwork mode.

n mode.

Things That Make You Go Zoom!

Illustrator lets you zoom in and out of your page, letting you view the entire page for layout, and giving you an up-close view for detail work. There are several ways to change the zoom percentage of a document.

☐ Use the Zoom tool. Select the Zoom tool from the Toolbox (see the following Time Saver) and click the place you want to zoom into; or even better, click and drag a marquee where you want to zoom (see Figure 1.24), and Illustrator tries to make that selected area fill the screen. Hold down the (Option)[Alt] key, and notice that the little plus sign inside the magnifying glass has turned to a minus sign, which will zoom out, letting you see more of your document, only smaller.

Figure 1.24.
Zooming in using the marquee method, as we did with the Selection tool.

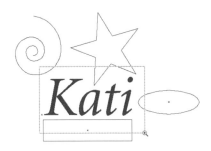

☐ Use the keyboard. (Command-hyphen)[Control-hyphen] will zoom out or down one increment, and (Command-=)[Control-=] will zoom in (or up) one increment.

☐ Select a custom view (see the section "Custom Views" later in this chapter).

TIME SAVER

To instantly access the Zoom tool at any time, no matter what tool you are using, simply press (Command-Spacebar)[Control-Spacebar], and your cursor will change to the magnifying glass. By *also* holding down the (Option)[Alt] key, you can zoom out, seeing more of your image. Upon releasing these keys, Illustrator brings you right back to the tool you were using.

Moving Around Your Page

When you zoom in really close to work on an image, there is only a small portion on the image visible. That's where the Hand tool (see Figure 1.25) comes into play. Select the Hand tool from the Toolbox. Press the mouse button and drag. The little hand "grabs" the page and moves it so you can see other parts of the image.

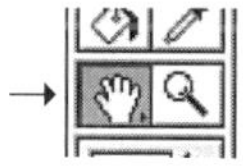

Figure 1.25.
The Hand tool.

TIME SAVER

To quickly zoom to fit your page in your document window, double-click the Hand tool. To quickly go to 100% magnification, double-click the Zoom tool.

Custom Views

If you work with large, complex images, you will be very happy that you took the time to read this chapter. I'll explain why. Everyone is always complaining about how slow computers are for graphics, and that you need expensive multiprocessor computers to keep up with today's work. Well, I'll let you in on a little secret. One of the biggest bottlenecks in computer graphics today is screen redraw. An accelerated graphics card can do wonders for your application speed. But Illustrator has a secret weapon that costs a lot less than a graphics accelerator: custom views.

Imagine yourself in a TV recording studio. There's one show that's happening on center stage, and they have five different cameras aimed at this stage. This gives the guy in the recording studio the ability to jump from camera to camera, seeing different views, instantaneously. Well, Illustrator's custom views work similarly.

To create a custom view, simply choose New View from the View menu (see Figure 1.26). Whatever your current view is, it will be automatically added to the Views list in the View menu. Attributes such as zoom percentage, viewing mode (Preview or Artwork), and window position are all saved, enabling you to quickly jump from an extreme close-up in Artwork mode, for example, to something such as a fit-in-window view in Preview mode. The first 10 views you define are also automatically assigned keyboard shortcuts—(Command-Option-Shift)[Control-Alt-Shift] and 1 through 0.

Figure 1.26.

Creating a new custom view.

New Window

Illustrator has a feature where you can create two different windows that contain the same artwork. It's the same file, but just viewed in two windows. You could, for example, work in Artwork mode in one window, and have another, smaller window in Preview mode, so you can see changes as you work.

To use this feature, choose New Window from the Window menu (see Figure 1.27), and a new window opens. Of course, whatever you do in one window automatically happens in the other.

Figure 1.27.

Creating a new window.

Another great way to use the New Window feature is if you have two monitors. By setting one of the monitors to 256 colors, you can see how your artwork will look if viewed at two different color settings. This can be very useful when designing art for the World Wide Web.

Context-Sensitive Menus

A new feature added to Illustrator 7 is *context-sensitive menus*. From anywhere on the screen, hold down the (Control key)[right mouse button] and click the screen. You will get a

1

pop-up list of the most common functions, depending on what you currently have selected (see Figure 1.28).

Figure 1.28.

Illustrator's new context-sensitive menus offer you a slew of relevant and usual commands, right where you want them, all at the touch of a key.

Summary

Congratulations! You've spent your first hour in Illustrator. There, that wasn't so bad now, was it? We learned how Illustrator is different from paint programs such as Photoshop, and we learned all about Illustrator's palettes and tools. Next hour, we will learn how to customize Illustrator to our needs and tastes, as well as learn how to set up a document to work in.

Term Review

Palettes—Small windows that contain settings such as colors or fonts.

Cross-platform—Terminology used to describe software that runs on multiple operating systems, such as Mac OS and Windows 95.

Raster image—A graphic consisting of a collection of dots, or pixels (see pixel).

Vector image—A graphic defined by a scalable, mathematical outline.

Pixel—A square that is the smallest part of an image; also called raster.

Pixelated—An image enlarged to the point where you can see the individual pixels.

Cursor—The icon on your screen that indicates the position of your mouse or selection point.

Focus—The active part of the screen. Because of all the new keyboard shortcuts in version 7, Illustrator might not know when you are entering data in a palette, or when you are trying to envoke a keyboard shortcut. By making a palette the active part of your screen — making it the focus — you are telling Illustrator exactly what you plan to do.

Floating palettes—A palette that is always visible (remains in front) even though the document window is selected.

Hour 2

Customizing Illustrator

When you move into a new house or apartment, you feel a kind of excitement, yet you also feel a bit uncomfortable because it's all new and different to you. Only after you've arranged things the way you like it, making adjustments and finding your favorite "spot," do you get that warm comfortable feeling.

The same holds true with Illustrator (although Illustrator is *a lot* cheaper than a new house). In the beginning, Illustrator may feel foreign—even overwhelming—but as you progress, you will find yourself getting comfortable working in Illustrator. One way of getting comfortable is setting Illustrator's preferences. In this chapter we learn about:

☐ Document Setup options

☐ Setting Illustrator preferences

☐ Using guides and grids

☐ Creating an Illustrator Startup file

Document Setup

The first step in creating a document is setting up the correct page size. Do this by selecting Document Setup from the File menu. You're presented with a dialog box with four sections: Artboard, View, Paths, and Options (see Figure 2.1).

Figure 2.1.

Illustrator's Document Setup dialog box.

Artboard

In the Artboard section, you specify the size of your page. You can choose from those listed in the Size pop-up menu, or you can enter a custom size manually—Illustrator supports page sizes anywhere from 2"×2" up to 120"×120"—in the Width and Height boxes. Clicking either Orientation icon swaps the width and height values, so you can quickly change from Portrait (tall) to Landscape (wide) format (see Figure 2.2).

Figure 2.2.

Simply clicking the Tall or Wide icon automatically swaps the width and height settings.

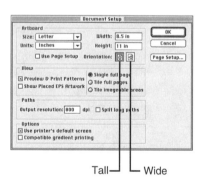

Tall—⌐ ⌐— Wide

You can select any of Illustrator's five supported measurement systems to specify page sizes by selecting one from the Units pop-up menu (see Figure 2.3). If you check the box marked Use Page Setup, Illustrator will use the page size that is currently selected in Page Setup. You can change the setting in Page Setup by clicking on the Page Setup button beneath the Cancel button.

Figure 2.3.

Selecting a measurement system.

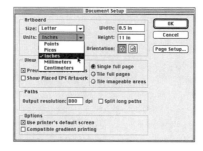

View

In the View section, you can choose to Preview & Print Patterns. Previewing patterns onscreen can slow down screen redraw considerably, and this option enables you to turn it off. You can also elect to Show Placed EPS Artwork. This setting is for when viewing placed images in Artwork mode, not Preview mode. You will always be able to see placed images in Preview mode.

Many times, Illustrator is used as a tool to create art that will then be placed into another program for final layout, such as PageMaker or QuarkXPress. In such cases, you don't need to create more than one page. When creating complex layouts and spreads, however, you can set Illustrator to create a number of pages in your document. Unlike other programs, however, Illustrator makes multiple pages in a document by splitting one large page into smaller pseudo-pages. You can either select Single full page, Tile full pages, which creates the most possible full-sized pages on your artboard (see Figure 2.4), or you can select Tile imageable areas, where Illustrator creates tiles to fill the entire artboard (see Figure 2.5).

Figure 2.4.

Only two 8 1/2"×11" pages fit onto this 20"×20" artboard using the Tile full pages option.

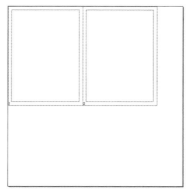

Figure 2.5.

Using the Tile imageable areas option, Illustrator maps out tiles for the entire 20"×20" artboard.

Paths

In the Paths section, you can choose a printer resolution, which helps Illustrator determine smooth gradients and clean curves, plus you have the option to Split long paths. What that means is that sometimes paths become very long and complex, filled with many *anchor points* (anchor points are part of a Bézier object, as we will learn later on). When a path has so many points, its complexity could cause problems at print time (see Figure 2.6). In such cases, in order to print the file, you can have Illustrator split the one big path into several smaller ones, which would make printing them possible (see Figure 2.7). Always save and keep a copy of your file *before* you split long paths, for future editing purposes—once a path is split, it is difficult to edit it.

Figure 2.6.

For demonstration purposes, a path with several hundred unnecessary anchor points has been created. This image will "choke" on an imagesetter and will not print.

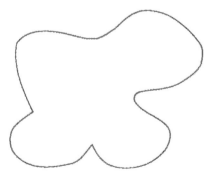

Options

In the Options section, you can choose to use the printer's default line screen setting, or, if you're printing to a Postscript Level 1 device, check the box marked Compatible gradient printing (if you're not sure about this, leave it unchecked, and if you have problems printing a file, try turning it on).

2

Figure 2.7.

After selecting Split long paths, saving the file, closing it, and reopening the file, you can see how Illustrator has split up the one large object into several smaller ones, and, more importantly, made the file printable.

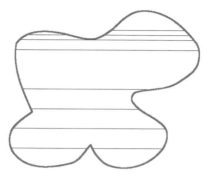

JUST A MINUTE

Any settings that you set in the Document Setup dialog box, or those that you will be setting in the Preferences dialog box (coming up next), are changeable at any time, even after you've saved it, closed it, and opened it again. Changes will take effect when you close either dialog box, except for the Split long paths option, which takes effect only when you save and close the file, and then reopen it.

Setting Preferences

Okay, so we've decided where all of the furniture goes, but there's still more to do. As I've come to realize, it's the smaller things in life that really make a difference in our daily lives. It isn't the bed or the refrigerator that gives that homey feeling, it's the rug on the floor or that cute little end table with the lava lamp on it. It's the pictures and paintings on the walls and the potpourri in the bathroom that creates a comfortable, safe feeling.

As we set Illustrator's preferences to our tastes, we will be creating our own little environment—our custom workspace—which enables us to use Illustrator comfortably, as well as conveniently.

Illustrator has six screens of preferences, all located in the Preferences dialog box, found in the File menu (see Figure 2.8). The six screens are General, Keyboard Increments, Units & Undo, Guides & Grid, Hyphenation Options, and Plug-ins & Scratch Disk.

To cycle through each of the six preferences screens, you can either select them from the pop-up menu at the top of the Preferences dialog box or you can use the Previous and Next buttons found on the far right of the dialog box (see Figure 2.9).

Figure 2.8.

*Choosing Preferences
from the File menu.*

Figure 2.9.

*Selecting a preference
screen from the pop-up
menu. Also notice the
Previous and Next
buttons on the far right.*

General Preferences

General Preferences has two sections: Tool Behavior and Options (see Figure 2.10).

Figure 2.10.

*The General Preferences
dialog box.*

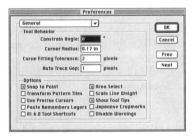

Tool Behavior

Constrain Angle is a really cool feature that sets the default angle of your document, which means if you set the angle to 30 degrees and draw a square while holding the Shift key, the square is drawn on a 30-degree angle. This is a great feature for creating 3D drawings, as well as for creating isometric drawings.

The Corner Radius is set here, which is used when drawing with the Rounded Rectangle tool. This setting can be overridden when drawing the rectangle (see Hour 3, "Drawing Basic Objects"), and the number here is only the default setting.

Curve Fitting Tolerance is used to determine how smooth or jagged a path is when drawn with the Freehand tool. The higher the setting, the smoother the path is (see Figure 2.11).

Figure 2.11.

The line on top was drawn with a Curve Fitting Tolerance of 2, the bottom one with a setting of 10.

Auto Trace Gap is used to determine where Illustrator ends a path when doing an autotrace.

Options

Snap to Point is one of Illustrator's most underrated features. This setting makes every point in an illustration work like a guide and makes working and moving items easy.

When performing transformations on objects, you can choose to Transform Pattern Tiles as well as the object (see Figure 2.12). Say you have a square that is filled with a pattern, for example. If you have Transform Pattern Tiles activated, and then you scale the square, the pattern fill scales as well. But if you have Transform Pattern Tiles turned off, the scale function resizes the square, but the pattern tiles remains the same size. This setting is only a default and can be overridden from within a transformation dialog box.

Figure 2.12.

The box on the right is the original item, and the center box has been rotated without Transform Pattern Tiles selected. The third box was rotated with Transform Pattern Tiles selected.

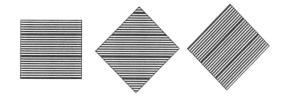

You can choose to Use Precise Cursors, which replaces Illustrator's tool cursors with crosshairs, allowing for more precise control. You can toggle this setting to see the standard cursors while working by using the Caps Lock key. If Use Precise Cursors is not checked, then pressing Caps Lock while working changes the cursor to a crosshair cursor.

Paste Remembers Layers keeps layer information intact when moving artwork to and from the Clipboard. You can set this from within the Layers palette as well.

AI 6.0 Tool Shortcuts is applicable only to the Macintosh platform. As of Illustrator 7, several keyboard shortcuts were changed to keep things consistent across computer platforms. For those people who want to keep with the "old way," selecting this option activates those shortcuts.

Area Select enables you to specify how Illustrator selects objects via the selection tools. With Area Select turned on, you can select objects by clicking anywhere within the object (if it is filled). With Area Select turned off, you must click the point or border of an object to select it (see Figure 2.13).

Figure 2.13.

The box on the left is being selected with Area Select activated, whereas the box on the right is being selected with Area Select deactivated.

Scale Line Weight determines whether Stroke weights are scaled when you transform objects. In other words, with Scale Line Weight activated, enlarging a box with a 1 pt. rule to 200% results in a box with a 2 pt. rule. With Scale Line Weight turned off, the rule remains at 1 point.

Did you forget the keyboard shortcut for that tool? Or did you forget which tool was the Scale tool? Illustrator makes it easy with Tool Tips. When activated (the default is set with Tool Tips on), simply drag your mouse over a tool and wait a second. A little teeny window pops up, telling you the name of the tool or function, and it also lists the keystroke command, if there is one.

Japanese Cropmarks are simply a different kind of crop mark, obviously used in Japan.

If you've used Illustrator before, you probably got those annoying dialog boxes that tell you that you can't do certain operations or functions (which was usually because you clicked just a few pixels too far). Well, Disable Warnings sends those dialog boxes home crying, and Illustrator will then alert you with a simple beep, upon encountering any violations.

Keyboard Increments

The Options section in Keyboard Increments refines how some keyboard shortcuts for type controls are implemented (see Figure 2.14). You can enter numerical input using any of Illustrator's measurement systems.

Figure 2.14.

The Keyboard Increments Preferences dialog box.

2

Options

The mouse is a nice little gadget, but when it comes to positioning something precisely, it can be a bit difficult to control. That's why Illustrator lets you *nudge* objects by using the arrows on your keyboard. The Cursor Key setting determines just how much each nudge is.

Size/Leading (pronounced "ledding") specifies how much leading is added or removed from a line of type when using the leading keyboard shortcut (Option-up arrow and Option-down arrow)[Alt-up arrow and Alt-down arrow].

Baseline Shift specifies the increment when using the *Baseline Shift* keyboard shortcut (Option-Shift-up arrow and Option-Shift-down arrow)[Alt-Shift-up arrow and Alt-Shift-down arrow].

The Tracking increment, measured in em's (literally, the width of the letter "M") determines the amount of tracking added or removed when applying the tracking keyboard shortcut (Option-left arrow, Option-right arrow)[Alt-left arrow, Alt-right arrow].

The Greeking Type Limit sets the size at which text is *greeked*. When small type is rendered onscreen, the computer has to work hard to calculate the letterforms. Because very small type is not readable onscreen anyway, the computer "greeks" the type by simply drawing gray bars where the type should appear (see Figure 2.15). Of course, if you zoom in closer, Illustrator renders the type correctly. Type greeking applies only to the screen, and when printing, all text appears correctly.

Figure 2.15.

The three gray bars are greeked text.

Hello There!
How Are you?

With Anti-alias Type turned on, type appears onscreen with smooth soft edges (see Figure 2.16). Usually, text appears jagged onscreen because of a computer monitor's low screen resolution (72 dpi). This setting is purely aesthetic and has no bearing when you print your file, for all type prints with smooth sharp edges from your PostScript printer. This should not be confused with anti-aliasing for web and raster images—we'll cover that in Hour 23, "Web Graphics."

Figure 2.16.

The word on top has anti-aliasing turned on; the word below had anti-aliasing turned off and appears jagged onscreen.

Antialias
Antialias

Basically the same as Area Select, mentioned earlier, with Type Area Select active, you can select type by clicking anywhere within the bounding box of the type (see the following Just a Minute). With Type Area Select turned off, you can only select type by selecting it on the baseline (see Figure 2.17).

Figure 2.17.

The word above has the type bounding box visible, and clicking anywhere within it with Type Area Select selects the word. The word below shows the type's baseline, which you must click to select type if Type Area Select is turned off.

JUST A MINUTE

When using the Baseline Shift option with type, keep in mind that although you can't see it, the bounding box still takes up all the space, and clicking what might seem like white space selects the type. Of course, only the type prints. By the same token, when selecting type by the baseline, if a baseline shift was applied, the baseline may be well above or below the type. In these cases, it is easiest to select the type when in Artwork mode.

Units & Undo

Rather straightforward, the Units & Undo dialog box contains two sections: Units and Undo (see Figure 2.18).

Figure 2.18.

The Units & Undo Preferences dialog box.

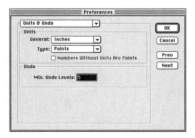

Units

Illustrator can use five different measurement systems—inches, millimeters, centimeters, picas, and points. You can set Illustrator to use any of these.

You can also enter any mathematical function within any of Illustrator's palettes and dialog boxes, and Illustrator does the math for you on the fly. You can also mix measurement systems in dialog boxes. You can, for example, enter 4 in. + 3p2 - 12mm, and Illustrator automatically does the math for you.

We will be doing several exercises later in the chapter, so it would be a good idea to set Illustrator's units to Inches for now.

TIME SAVER

Here's a tip for Macintosh users: If you're working with one measurement system, and you want to quickly switch to another, press Command-Control-U to toggle through all five measurement systems. This works directly in the document, and there is no need to open the Preferences dialog box.

Undo

Hey, we all make mistakes sometimes, and that's okay because Illustrator has *multiple undos.* Just how many, you ask? Well, that depends on how much RAM you have allocated to Illustrator. Illustrator keeps track of as many undos as memory allows, but it never goes below the amount that you set here. But remember, the more undos you have, the less RAM Illustrator has for other things. Illustrator's default setting is 5, and unless you're working on really large files, I don't recommend using anything higher than 10.

Guides & Grid

An important feature of almost any program, Guides & Grid helps you easily align objects and create perfect layouts and art. Guides are vertical or horizontal lines that you can place anywhere on your page. These guides will not print; they are only visible onscreen. The grid is similar to graph paper—a set of non-printing boxes that fill your page, making for easier layout. The Guides & Grid Preferences dialog box contains two sections: Guides and Grid (see Figure 2.19).

Figure 2.19.

The Guides & Grid Preferences dialog box.

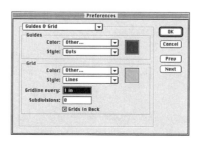

You can specify what color guides should be either by choosing from the pop-up list of pre-defined colors Illustrator provides or by choosing Other and selecting any other color from the Color Picker. You also have the option of having Illustrator render guides as solid lines or dotted lines.

You have the same options with Illustrator's Grid settings as you had with Guides. You can choose any color that pleases you, as well as specify a solid or dotted line.

You can also specify how the grid is drawn up, with main gridlines at any increment, and multiple subdivisions.

Working with Guides and Illustrator's Grid

If you've worked in any page layout program, such as PageMaker or QuarkXPress, you know how important guides are. They help in layout and design and for aligning objects.

As guides and the grid are important, I would like to leave the preferences alone for a moment and talk about how to use these features in Illustrator. If you have the Preferences dialog box open, please close it, as we will be working in Illustrator for a little while.

Rulers

When Illustrator opens, you are presented with a new blank file. Let's turn on our rulers. From the View menu, select Show Rulers (see Figure 2.20). Notice that your rulers appear across the top and left side of your screen. If you set them earlier, they should be set in inches. If not, Mac users can use the keyboard shortcut (Command-Control-U) to toggle over to inches; Windows users will have to return to Preferences and choose Inches in the Units & Undo screen.

Figure 2.20.

Turning Illustrator's rulers on. I still wonder why Adobe doesn't have Illustrator launch with rulers on as a default.

Creating Guides

Creating guides in Illustrator is really simple.

1. Drag your mouse so that your cursor is directly on the ruler (see Figure 2.21).

2. Press and drag the mouse onto the artboard.

3. When you've positioned your guide, release the mouse button.

2

Figure 2.21.

*Preparing to drag
out a guide.*

In its default setting, guides are always locked. After you've placed them, you cannot select them, move them, or delete them. To do so, you must unlock the guides by choosing Lock Guides (Command-Option-;)[Control-Alt-;] from the View menu (see Figure 2.22).

Figure 2.22.

*Choosing Lock Guides
toggles between locked
and unlocked guides.*

You can also turn any Illustrator object (such as a square, a star, or an ellipse) into a guide by simply selecting it and choosing Make Guides (Command-5)[Control-5] from the View menu (see Figure 2.23). You can return a guide back to its original state as an object by selecting it, and then choosing Release Guides (Command-Option-5)[Control-Alt-5] from the View menu.

Figure 2.23.

*Making an Illustrator
object into a guide.*

Illustrator's Grid

A new and welcome addition to Illustrator 7 is the Grid feature. Turn the grid on by selecting Show Grid from the View menu (see Figure 2.24). Your screen should now look like a sheet of graph paper. To change how the grid appears, select Guides & Grid from the Preferences submenu, as we mentioned before.

Figure 2.24.

Turning on Illustrator's grid.

TIME SAVER

Besides helping with layout, Illustrator's grid serves another great purpose. With the grid as the backmost object (which you can set in Preferences), you can quickly tell whether an object is filled with None, or white.

Snap To Grid

The grid is nice, but what makes it powerful is that Illustrator snaps to it. Gridlines act as a kind of magnet, and your mouse "sticks" to them when it gets near them. Sometimes this can get annoying, though, and you can turn off the Snap To feature by choosing Snap To Grid from the View menu (see Figure 2.25).

Figure 2.25.

The Snap To Grid toggle in the View menu.

Okay! You've learned how to work with guides and the grid, so let's get back to the rest of Illustrator's preferences. On with the show!

Hyphenation

Rather simple, the Hyphenation Options screen of the Preferences dialog box lets you select a default language, as well as add and delete entries into the dictionary (see Figure 2.26).

Figure 2.26.

The Hyphenation Options screen of the Preferences dialog box.

Plug-ins & Scratch Disk

In this dialog box (see Figure 2.27), there are two sections: Plug-ins Folder and Scratch Disks.

Figure 2.27.

The Plug-ins & Scratch Disk Preferences dialog box.

Plug-ins Folder

The Plug-ins folder is where Illustrator keeps all of its "extensions" or add-ons, including third-party filters and plug-ins. There might be times when Illustrator "loses touch" with its Plug-ins folder. If this happens, you'll need to remind Illustrator where the Plug-ins folder is. You may also want to keep more than one Plug-ins folder, and this dialog box enables you to switch between the two.

To specify the Plug-ins folder:

1. Under the File menu, select Preferences (Command-K)[Control-K].
2. From the pop-up menu, select Plug-ins & Scratch Disk.
3. Click the Choose button to locate the Plug-ins folder.
4. Click OK.
5. Quit and relaunch Illustrator.

Scratch Disks

Those of you familiar with Photoshop are probably familiar with the term *scratch disk.* A scratch disk is like Illustrator's scrap paper, where it temporarily holds data to perform operations. As the default, your scratch disk is your startup drive. When working with large files, your scratch disk can fill up rather quickly.

Illustrator lets you specify which disk should be the scratch disk, and it also enables you to specify a secondary scratch disk—where Illustrator goes if the primary scratch disk is full. If you have only one hard drive, you can specify a removable disk, such as a Syquest, Jaz, or Zip, to be your secondary scratch disk.

To specify a scratch disk:

1. Under the File menu, choose Preferences.
2. From the pop-up menu, choose Plug-ins & Scratch Disk.
3. Select a primary and a secondary scratch disk.
4. Click OK.

You will need to restart Illustrator for both plug-ins and scratch disk info to take effect.

Creating an Illustrator Start-up File

When you quit Illustrator, it "remembers" the position of the palettes, and the next time you open Illustrator, it looks just like it did when you quit it. But all of the other settings, such as colors, page size, which typeface is the default, and so on, are defined by a file called the Illustrator start-up file, and those settings revert to match the start-up file every time you launch Illustrator. Whatever is in this file appears whenever you launch Illustrator.

To create a customized Illustrator start-up file:

1. Create a document with whatever settings you'd like to make the default.
2. Save the file in Illustrator format, and name it "Adobe Illustrator Startup."
3. Place the file in the Illustrator Plug-ins folder.
4. Restart Illustrator.

Summary

We're learning more and more about Illustrator, and the dust is beginning to settle as we become more familiar with Illustrator's feel and metaphors. We learned how to customize Illustrator to tailor-fit our needs, and we learned how to set up a file, ready for use, with guides and grids. Next, we will begin learning how to draw simple shapes, using Illustrator's primary drawing tools.

Term Review

Artboard—Illustrator's term for the actual page you work on.

Gradient—An attribute referring to the blending of colors into each other.

Anchor point—The heart of a Bézier curve. More on this in Hour 6, "Drawing Bézier Paths."

Line screen—Printing term referring to the number of dots per inch.

Stroke weight—The stroke is the outline of a shape, and the weight refers to the thickness of the outline.

Transform—A function, such as scaling, rotating, or moving, performed on an object.

Nudge—The act of moving a selection incrementally using the keyboard arrow keys.

Leading—Typographical term for the space between lines of text.

Baseline shift—Typographical term for the vertical movement of text relative to the base.

Tracking—Typographical term for the addition or removal of space between letters.

Greeked type—Gray lines used to substitute for small type on screen.

Multiple undos—An undo is the act of deleting the last thing you just did, making as if it never happened (something we all need in real life). Multiple undos means you can go back several steps.

Plug-ins—Adobe or third-party add-ons or extra features for Illustrator. Extensis VectorTools is an example of a set of plug-ins.

Scratch disk—A temporary area on your hard drive that Illustrator uses to calculate operations.

2

Hour 3

Drawing Basic Objects

Now the fun begins—you actually start drawing something. You start with the easy shapes, such as rectangles and ovals, moving up to polygons, stars, spirals, and freeform objects. One of the great things about Illustrator is that there is usually more than one way to accomplish the same thing. As you progress, you get a feel of when using one technique might be better in certain situations than another. Specifically, this hour covers:

- ☐ Drawing rectangles and ellipses
- ☐ Drawing polygons, stars and spirals
- ☐ The Paintbrush tool
- ☐ Saving your work

TIME SAVER

Probably the most important thing about Illustrator—let me correct myself—the most important *things* about Illustrator are the modifier keys— Shift, (Option)[Alt], and (Command)[Control]. Using combinations of these keys when you are drawing with the mouse controls different options. It's important that you become familiar with these key combinations to the point where they become second nature, and you don't even think about them—you just do it.

Rectangles and Ellipses

The most primitive shapes, rectangles, and ellipses are also the easiest shapes to create in Illustrator. There are several ways of drawing these shapes, each a slight variant of the other, and as you work more in Illustrator, you get a better feel for when to use each method.

As we discussed in the first hour, Illustrator is a vector art program. A vector rectangle or ellipse consists of three things: a starting point, an ending point, and a center point. You define the start and end point and Illustrator calculates the center point for you automatically. They say the best way to learn is to do it yourself, so let's draw, shall we?

Drawing Rectangles

Let's start by drawing a rectangle.

1. Select the Rectangle tool (see Figure 3.1). Notice your cursor becomes a crosshair (see Figure 3.2).

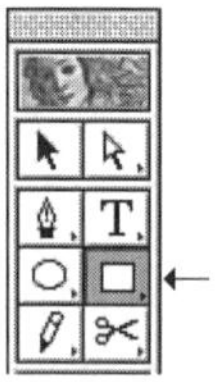

Figure 3.1.

The Rectangle tool.

Figure 3.2.

The Rectangle tool's cursor.

-|-

2. Position your cursor where you want the upper-left corner of the rectangle to be.
3. Click the mouse button, but don't let go. Drag down and to the right, and release the mouse button (see Figure 3.3).

3

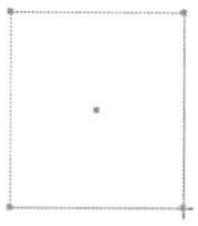

Figure 3.3.

Dragging to draw a rectangle.

Holding the Shift key while dragging forces your box, or *constrains* it, to be a perfect square—even on all sides. Throughout Illustrator, the Shift key is almost always the constrain key. Using it often takes the guesswork out of creating and manipulating your illustrations, as Illustrator does the work for you.

Using the Rounded Rectangle Tool

A rounded rectangle is one where the corners don't come to a point but are rounded. Now let's draw a rounded rectangle.

1. Select the Rounded Rectangle tool (see Figure 3.4).

Figure 3.4.

The Rounded Rectangle tool.

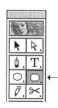

2. Position your cursor where you want the upper-left corner of the rounded rectangle to be.
3. Click the mouse button, but don't let go. Drag down and to the right (see Figure 3.5), and release the mouse button.

Figure 3.5.

Dragging to draw a rounded rectangle.

Holding the Shift key while dragging forces your rounded rectangle to have four even sides. To change the *corner radius* of the rounded rectangle, see "Drawing Rectangles Numerically," later in this hour.

Drawing Out From the Center

Until now, we have been drawing our shapes by starting from the upper-left corner and dragging to the lower-right corner. Illustrator can also draw shapes out from the center.

1. Select the Centered Rectangle tool (see Figure 3.6). Notice your cursor has changed to centered cross hairs (see Figure 3.7).

Figure 3.6.
*The Centered Rectangle
tool.*

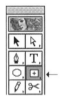

Figure 3.7.
*The Centered Rectangle
tool's cross-hair cursor.*

2. Position your cursor where you want the center of your rectangle to be.

3. Click the mouse button, but don't let go. Drag outwards (see Figure 3.8) and release the mouse button.

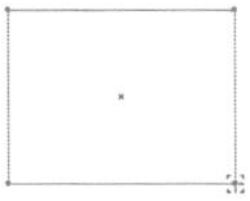

Figure 3.8.
*Dragging to draw a
rectangle out from the
center.*

The same technique applies to the Centered Rounded Rectangle tool (see Figure 3.9).

Figure 3.9.
*The Centered Rounded
Rectangle tool.*

TIME SAVER

If you have the Rectangle tool selected and you want to draw a box out from the center, hold down the (Option)[Alt] key before dragging. See how your cursor changes between the regular and centered cross hairs.

Drawing Rectangles Numerically

The previously mentioned ways of drawing a box are great when you want to draw something freely, but there are many times when you need to create a rectangle or square with exact proportions.

1. Select the desired rectangle creation tool.

3

2. Click the screen and let go of the mouse button. Illustrator presents you with a dialog box (see Figure 3.10).

Figure 3.10.

Drawing a rectangle numerically.

3. Enter the width and height (and corner radius if necessary) and click OK.

Depending on which tool you have selected, Illustrator draws the shape from either the center or the upper-left corner of where you clicked. Again, you can use the (Option)[Alt] key to quickly toggle between these two modes.

Ellipses

Ellipses (also known as ovals or circles) are slightly different than the rectangles we've been drawing. Whereas a rectangle is made up of four straight line segments, a circle is made up of four *curved* segments. In Hour 6, "Drawing Bézier Paths," we talk more in detail about straight and curved segments. Actually, drawing an ellipse in Illustrator is very similar to drawing a rectangle.

Now let's draw an ellipse.

1. Select the Ellipse tool (see Figure 3.11). Notice your cursor becomes a crosshair (see Figure 3.12).

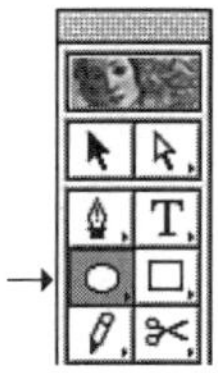

Figure 3.11.

The Ellipse tool.

Figure 3.12.

The cursor for the Ellipse tool.

2. Position your cursor where you want the upper-left edge of the ellipse to be.

3. Click the mouse button, but don't let go. Drag down and to the right and release the mouse button (see Figure 3.13).

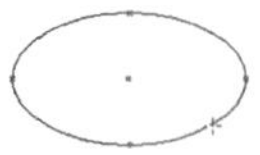

Figure 3.13.
Dragging to draw an ellipse.

Holding the Shift key while dragging constrains your ellipse to a perfect circle.

Drawing Out from the Center

You can also draw a circle from its center point.

1. Select the Centered Ellipse tool (see Figure 3.14). Notice your cursor has changed to centered crosshairs (see Figure 3.15).

Figure 3.14.
The Centered Ellipse tool.

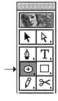

Figure 3.15.
The cursor indicating the Centered Ellipse tool is selected

2. Position your cursor where you want the center of your ellipse to be.
3. Click the mouse button, but don't let go. Drag outwards and release the mouse button (see Figure 3.16).

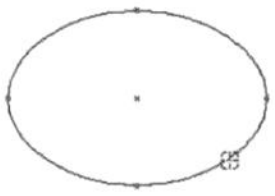

Figure 3.16.
Dragging to draw an ellipse out from the center.

Drawing an Ellipse Numerically

As with the rectangles, you can create an ellipse numerically.

1. Select the desired ellipse creation tool.
2. Click the screen and let go of the mouse button. Illustrator presents you with a dialog box (see Figure 3.17).
3. Enter the width and height and click OK.

3

Figure 3.17.

*Creating an ellipse
numerically.*

Depending on which tool you have selected, Illustrator draws the shape from either the center or the upper-left of where you clicked. Again, use the (Option)[Alt] key to quickly toggle between these two modes.

Great! Now that we can draw primitive shapes such as rectangles and ovals, let's move on to drawing more complex shapes. Of course, after you create a shape in Illustrator, you can edit it in all sorts of ways. We get to editing and transformations in Hours 7 and 12.

Drawing Other Shapes

The next three creation tools are really cool. They first appeared in Illustrator 6 as plug-in tools, in their own little palette. Now they are fully integrated into the interface (grouped with the Ellipse tool in the Toolbox), with all of their coolness intact. The three tools are the Polygon tool, the Star tool, and the Spiral tool. These *interactive tools* create complex shapes in a fraction of the time it would take to draw them manually.

The Polygon Tool

The Polygon tool is used to create shapes such as triangles, pentagons, and octagons (for those of you who like making stop signs).

1. Select the Polygon tool (see Figure 3.18). Notice the cursor is now a different, smaller crosshairs (see Figure 3.19).

Figure 3.18.

The Polygon tool.

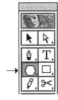

Figure 3.19.

*The cursor, indicating
the Polygon tool is
selected.*

2. The Polygon tool always draws out from the center. Click the mouse button, and drag outwards (see Figure 3.20). Do not let go of the mouse button until the last step of this exercise.

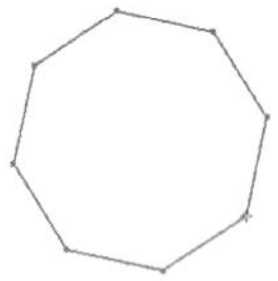

Figure 3.20.

Dragging to draw a polygon.

3. Rotate the polygon by moving your mouse in a circular motion (see Figure 3.21).

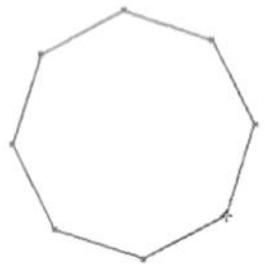

Figure 3.21.

Rotating the polygon in real time as you're creating it.

4. Add more sides to the polygon by pressing the up arrow key on your keyboard (see Figure 3.22). If you hold the key down, it adds sides repeatedly.

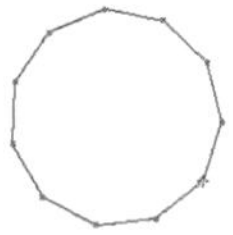

Figure 3.22.

Adding sides to your polygon.

5. Remove sides from the polygon by pressing the down arrow key on your keyboard (see Figure 3.23). Holding the key removes sides repeatedly.

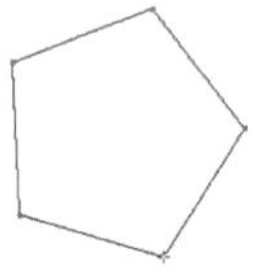

Figure 3.23.

Removing sides from your polygon.

6. To keep the polygon straight (constrained at 90° or whatever the Constrain Angle is set to in Preferences), press the Shift key.

7. Press the Spacebar, and the polygon "freezes," enabling you to move the mouse and position the polygon on the page.

8. The tilde key (~) creates duplicates of the polygon as you drag and move it.

9. Release the mouse button.

You can use any combination of the modifier keys simultaneously as you create your polygon.

Creating a Polygon Numerically

You can also create a polygon numerically.

1. Select the Polygon tool.

2. Click the mouse button. Illustrator presents you with a dialog box (see Figure 3.24).

Figure 3.24.

Creating a polygon numerically.

3. Enter the radius size and the number of sides.

4. Click OK.

The Star Tool

The Star tool is one of the great time-savers. It used to be a real drag to create stars and starbursts—now it really is just a drag!

1. Select the Star tool (see Figure 3.25).

Figure 3.25.

The Star tool.

2. Stars are always drawn from the center. Click the mouse button and drag outwards (see Figure 3.26). Do not let go of the mouse button until the end of this exercise.

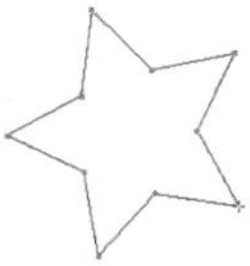

Figure 3.26.

Dragging to create a star.

3. Rotate the star as you are dragging it by moving the mouse in a circular motion (see Figure 3.27).

Figure 3.27.

Rotating the star in real time, as you draw it.

4. Press the up arrow key to add points to the star (see Figure 3.28).

Figure 3.28.

Adding points to your star.

5. Press the down arrow key to remove points from the star (see Figure 3.29).

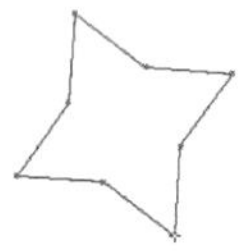

Figure 3.29.

Removing points from your star.

6. Press the Shift key to keep the star straight and aligned with the baseline.
7. Press the (Option)[Alt] key to align the segments on either side of each point—the point's shoulders—with each other so that they form a straight line (see Figure 3.30).

Figure 3.30.

Aligning the shoulders on your star.

8. Press the (Command)[Control] key to adjust the inner radius of the star (see Figure 3.31). This controls how "pointy" the star is.

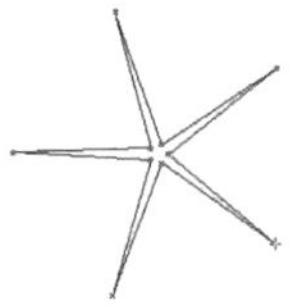

Figure 3.31.

Changing the inner and outer radius with the (Command)[Control] key.

9. Press and hold the Spacebar to "freeze" the star, and position it on the page.
10. Press the tilde key to make numerous copies of your star as you drag (see Figure 3.32).

3

Figure 3.32.

This was created by holding down the Option, Shift, Spacebar, and tilde keys simultaneously, while dragging the mouse.

You can use any combination of the modifier keys simultaneously as you create your star.

Creating a Star Numerically

You can also create a star numerically.

1. Select the Star tool.

2. Click the mouse and release the button to bring up the dialog box shown in Figure 3.33.

Figure 3.33.

Drawing a star numerically.

3. Enter values for the outer and inner radius (Radius 1 and 2, respectively) and the number of points. The outer radius, Radius 1, is where the points facing outwards extend to, whereas the inner radius, Radius 2, is where the points facing inward extend to.

4. Click OK.

The Spiral Tool

There was a time when drawing spirals was very difficult, but it's easy now thanks to the Spiral tool. By simply clicking and dragging, you can create interesting spirals while controlling the number of winds (how many times it goes around) and attributes, such as whether the spiral goes clockwise or counterclockwise. Do not confuse the Spiral tool with the Twirl tool, which looks similar. We'll cover the Twirl tool later in the book.

1. Select the Spiral tool (see Figure 3.34).

2. Spirals are always drawn from the center. Click the mouse button and drag outwards (see Figure 3.35). Do not let go of the mouse button until the end of this exercise.

Figure 3.34.

The Spiral tool.

Figure 3.35.

Dragging to create a spiral.

3. Rotate the spiral as you are dragging it by moving the mouse in a circular motion (see Figure 3.36).

Figure 3.36.

Rotating the spiral as you draw.

4. Press the up arrow key to add segments (or winds) to the spiral (see Figure 3.37).

Figure 3.37.

Adding segments to your spiral.

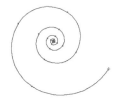

5. Press the down arrow key to remove segments from the spiral (see Figure 3.38).

Figure 3.38.

Removing segments from your spiral.

6. Press the Shift key to constrain the rotation of the spiral to 45 degree increments.

7. Press the (Option)[Alt] key to control the style of the spiral. This determines whether the winds go to the right or the left.

3

8. Press the (Command)[Control] key to adjust the decay of the spiral (see Figure 3.39). This controls how far "into the distance" the spiral goes.

Figure 3.39.

Adjusting the decay of the spiral with the (Command)[Control] Key.

9. Press and hold the Spacebar to "freeze" the spiral, and position it on the page.
10. Pressing the tilde key makes numerous copies of your spiral as you drag (see Figure 3.40).

Figure 3.40.

Many spirals can look like waves.

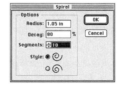

You can use any combination of the modifier keys simultaneously as you create your spiral.

Creating a Spiral Numerically

You can also create a spiral numerically.

1. Select the Spiral tool.
2. Click the mouse and release the button to bring up the dialog box shown in Figure 3.41.

Figure 3.41.

Creating a spiral numerically.

3. Enter values for the radius, decay, and segments and choose a style (clockwise or counterclockwise).
4. Click OK.

The Paintbrush Tool

Until now, we have been drawing predefined, symmetrical shapes. Now we move into the world of freedom—creating freeform shapes with the Paintbrush tool (see Figure 3.42).

Figure 3.42.

The Paintbrush tool.

Drawing with the Paintbrush tool is easy. Just select the tool, press the mouse button, and drag. Let go of the mouse button as you complete each stroke in your drawing.

The Paintbrush is actually creating a filled object in the shape you draw.

When using the Paintbrush, there are several options that can change the way your drawing looks. Double-click the Paintbrush tool in the Toolbox, and Illustrator presents you with the Paintbrush Options dialog box (see Figure 3.43).

Figure 3.43.

The different options available with the Paintbrush tool. Variable width is grayed out if you do not have a pressure-sensitive tablet installed.

You can give the Paintbrush a calligraphic style for effect (see Figure 3.44). You can also change the line caps and joins (see Figure 3.45). But the most powerful feature of the Paintbrush tool is the ability to change the width of your shapes. If you have a pressure-sensitive drawing tablet, you can set a variable width, and the harder you press as you draw, the thicker your shape is (see Figure 3.46). If you do not have a pressure-sensitive tablet, you are only able to set a fixed width.

Figure 3.44.
This shape was created in one stroke, with the Paintbrush's calligraphic option turned on.

Figure 3.45.
The top shape was created with rounded caps and rounded joins, while the lower shape was created with square caps and mitered joins.

3

Save Your Work

No doubt, after this lesson, you created a masterpiece that you want to keep forever, so let's save your work.

1. Choose Save from the File menu,
2. Give the file a name and click OK.

You just learned to save a file. The very nature of a computer is to crash when you least expect it to, and when you are relying on it most. It's a good idea to get into the habit of saving your files frequently and keeping backups of them in case you lose them or they become corrupt.

Figure 3.46.

Using the Variable Width setting with a pressure-sensitive tablet, you can create a shape with natural-looking, hand-drawn thicks and thins.

Summary

Your feet are definitely wet, as you learned to draw simple shapes. You had fun creating polygons and using the Paintbrush tool, and you learned the power of using the modifier keys as you draw. Next, you begin to learn to edit and manipulate the shapes you created today.

Term Review

Modifier keys—The Shift, Control, (Option)[Alt], and (Command)[Control] keys found on your keyboard.

Corner radius—The amount of curve at the corners of a rounded rectangle.

Interactive tools—Tools that let you change options on-the-fly as you are drawing with them.

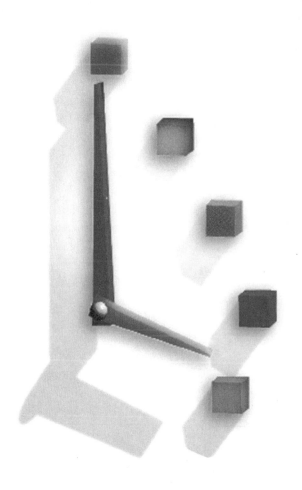

Hour **4**

Working with Selections

Besides actually drawing your illustration, the most important things to master in Illustrator are the selection tools. Please allow me to explain. Illustrator can do lots of things, but it has to know where and when to do them. Let's say you have a picture of a face. If you want to make the eyes smaller, you have to select the eyes before you perform the transformation, or Illustrator will scale the whole face. By selecting only certain objects, or even just certain parts of an object, we can tell Illustrator exactly what we want it to do and, more importantly, have complete control over our file (see Figure 4.1). In this chapter we talk all about selecting objects, including:

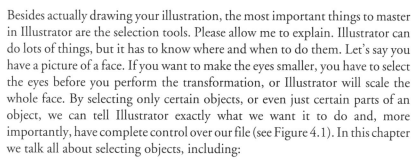

- ☐ The selection tools
- ☐ Grouping objects
- ☐ Locking and hiding objects
- ☐ Arranging objects

Figure 4.1.

The image on the left is the original. The middle is what happens when you scale the entire illustration, and the image on the right had just the eyes reduced.

The Selection Tools

There are three selection tools: the Selection tool, the Direct Selection tool, and the Group Selection tool. We'll discuss each of them in detail, as well as learn to use each of them effectively.

The Selection Tool

The Selection tool (or the black arrow, as it is most commonly called because of its appearance) is used to select entire objects (see Figure 4.2). You select an object simply by clicking it (see the section "Area Select," later in this chapter). After an object is selected, you can move it by clicking the mouse button and dragging the object.

Figure 4.2.

The Selection tool, also referred to as the black arrow.

Let's give the Selection tool a whirl, shall we? Make sure you have Illustrator open, and if you don't already have an empty file opened, select New (Command-N)[Control-N] from the File menu (see Figure 4.3).

Figure 4.3.

Creating a new document.

4

1. Press D to set your colors to the default setting of a white fill and a black stroke. Don't worry, we'll go into detail about fills and strokes in Hours 10, "Fills," and 11, "Strokes."

2. Draw several rectangles on your page (see Figure 4.4).

Figure 4.4.

Your screen should look something like this.

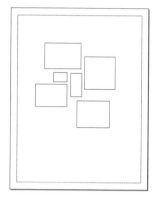

3. After you have drawn the last rectangle, choose the Selection tool from the Toolbox.

4. Click any rectangle. Notice that the object has become selected (see Figure 4.5). You can see the four anchor points of the rectangle, and its Bézier path has become highlighted in light blue (when we discuss Layers in the next hour, we'll talk more about what color selected objects are).

Figure 4.5.

The selected rectangle.

5. Now that the rectangle is selected, click and drag the rectangle to move it to a new position (see Figure 4.6). Release the mouse button when you have moved the rectangle to its new home.

Figure 4.6.

Dragging the rectangle to move it.

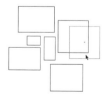

6. Deselect the rectangle by clicking any blank space on the page.

Now let's select and move more than one object at a time.

1. Click any rectangle to select it.

2. Press and hold down the Shift key.

3. Click another rectangle to add it to your selection (see Figure 4.7).

Figure 4.7.

With the first rectangle still selected, clicking the second rectangle while pressing the Shift key will add the second rectangle to your selection.

4. Now click and drag one of the rectangles, and both selected rectangles move together (see Figure 4.8).

Figure 4.8.

Moving both rectangles simultaneously.

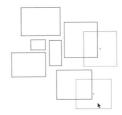

5. Deselect the rectangles by pressing (Command-Shift-A)[Control-Shift-A], or by clicking any blank space on the page.

JUST A MINUTE

The Shift key is actually a toggle that adds or subtracts from your selection. In the previous example, we selected rectangle number one and then selected rectangle number two while holding down the Shift key. Now, with both rectangles selected, if you were to Shift-select rectangle number two *again*, it would become *deselected* (go ahead and try it). The Shift key makes an unselected item selected, or a selected item unselected.

The Shift key technique can really save time when making certain selections, too, as in the following exercise, where we will try to select all the rectangles except for the one in the middle. From what we've learned until now, you would Shift-select each rectangle until all

4

were selected except the one in the center. Depending on how many rectangles you have, that could be a lot of work! Now let's do it in two easy steps:

1. Using the same rectangles as the above exercise, press (Command-A)[Control-A] to select all.

2. Hold down the Shift button and, using the Selection tool, click the center rectangle.

Sure, this may not seem like such a big deal now, when we have just a few rectangles on our page, but imagine if we had fifty, or even a hundred rectangles. Imagine how much time you'd save *then*.

There is yet another way to select objects, and this one is called the marquee method, which defines a selection by drawing a bounding box around what we want selected. Anything that falls within the bounding box becomes selected. We will continue to work on the same file with all our rectangles, as I am becoming rather fond of them.

1. Click any blank area onscreen or press (Command-Shift-A)[Control-Shift-A] to make sure that nothing is selected.

2. Position your mouse to the upper left of the object(s) you want to select (see Figure 4.9).

Figure 4.9.

Position the mouse to begin the marquee.

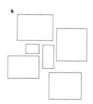

3. Press and drag the mouse down and to the right. As you drag, a dotted line appears (see Figure 4.10). Any object that falls within this "bounding box" is selected. If there are multiple objects, you do *not* need to hold down the Shift key.

Figure 4.10.

Defining the marquee.

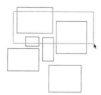

4. Release the mouse button, and the objects are selected (see Figure 4.11).

Figure 4.11.

The selected objects.

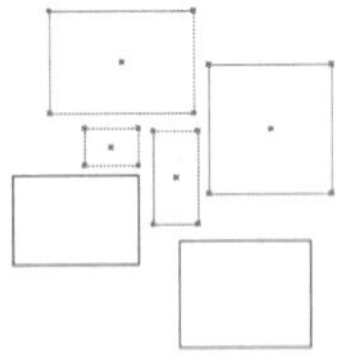

Sometimes, using the marquee method saves a lot of time, too, as in the case we presented earlier, when trying to select all rectangles except for the middle one. You can marquee-select all the rectangles, and then Shift-click the center one to deselect it. This is especially useful when working on one portion of a page, where using (Command-A)[Control-A] would select other unwanted objects.

The Direct Selection Tool

The Direct Selection tool, or as I like to call it, the white arrow, is the selection tool used the most in Illustrator (see Figure 4.12). In a few moments, you will see why. As we just learned, the black arrow is used to select entire objects. The white arrow, on the other hand, is used to select *parts* of an object. Although we could only move an entire object with the black arrow, the white arrow enables us to move parts of an object, individually.

Figure 4.12.

The Direct Selection tool.

Let's go back to our file with all the rectangles and try to move a single point.

1. Click any blank area on the screen or press (Command-Shift-A)[Control-Shift-A] to make sure that nothing is selected.
2. Choose the Direct Selection tool from the Toolbox.
3. Carefully select the lower-right corner of one of the rectangles (see Figure 4.13).

Figure 4.13.

When you select just one corner, notice that the selected point you clicked on is solid, whereas the other, unselected points are hollow.

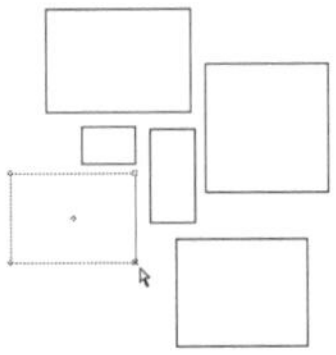

4

4. Press and drag down and to the right. Notice that only the point that you selected is moving—the rest of the object stands still (see Figure 4.14). Release the mouse button.

Figure 4.14.

Moving part of an object.

Let's try something a little different now and move a single line segment:

1. Carefully move your mouse right over the edge of one of the rectangles (see Figure 4.15).

Figure 4.15.

Selecting just one of the rectangle's line segments.

2. Press and drag outwards (see Figure 4.16). Notice how just the one side moves.

Figure 4.16.

Moving the line is really like moving two points with one click.

3. Press and hold the Shift key as you drag to constrain your move to 45° angles.

You're doing great! Now let's apply what we've learned up to now and move multiple points:

1. Click and select one of the corners (anchor points) of a rectangle.

2. Now hold down the Shift key and click the anchor point directly opposite that point (see Figure 4.17).

Figure 4.17.

Using Shift-click to add anchor points to the selection.

3. Click and drag one of the points. Because both points are selected, they both move as you drag (see Figure 4.18).

Figure 4.18.

Moving both selected points.

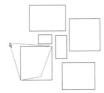

4. Release the mouse button.

Marquee selecting works here as well. Let's try it.

1. Deselect any objects by pressing (Command-Shift-A)[Control-Shift-A].

2. Marquee-select the bottom two points of a rectangle (see Figure 4.19).

3. Press and drag on one of the points.

Figure 4.19.

Marquee-selecting multiple anchor points.

Great! Now that we are familiar with the black and white arrows, we can go on to grouping objects, and we'll learn about the Group Selection tool, which is a variation of the white arrow. I mentioned before that the white arrow is the most used selection tool in Illustrator, and if you hang in there just a few more minutes, you'll see the light.

Grouping Objects

Let's have a little fun, shall we? Create a new document by choosing New from the File menu. Draw 10 rectangles randomly throughout the screen. Now draw 10 circles (see Figure 4.20).

4

Okay, now imagine you are showing this incredible work of art to your boss. I can just hear him say it now: *"That's not what I wanted! I want you to shift all the circles over one inch to the left!"*

Figure 4.20.

Picasso would be proud.

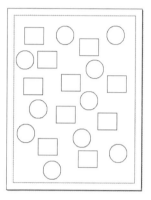

He leaves in a huff, and now you must make a change. So we begin the wonderful task of moving each circle one inch to the left—a time-consuming task, I assure you. So what do we do? I was *hoping* you'd ask that question…

1. Using the black arrow, select one circle (see Figure 4.21).

Figure 4.21.

Selecting the first circle.

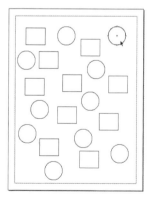

2. While holding down the Shift key, click and select the rest of the circles (see Figure 4.22).

3. Choose Group from the Object menu (see Figure 4.23).

Figure 4.22.

Selecting the remaining circles while holding the Shift key.

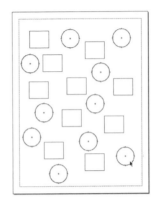

Figure 4.23.

Choosing Group from the Object menu.

You've just created a *group!* To see what you've actually done, deselect everything (Command-Shift-A)[Control-Shift-A] and then, using the black arrow, select just one of the circles. You'll be pleasantly surprised to see that all the circles have now become selected. It is now easy to move all the circles together. In fact, anticipating even more changes from our favorite boss, it might be a good idea to group the rectangles as well. But before we begin selecting all our rectangles, I think I feel another step-by-step coming on...

1. From the Edit menu, choose Select All (Command-A)[Control-A].
2. While holding down the Shift key, click a circle.

All the rectangles are selected. Because the circles are a group, deselecting one of them deselected all of them. Now would be a good time to group the rectangles by pressing (Command-G)[Control-G].

Groups are extremely helpful when you are working in complex documents, and it's a good idea to group items as you create them. After creating a logo, for instance, group it. This way you can move it around easily, and more importantly, you won't accidentally lose parts by trying to select each and every piece, every time (inevitably, you'll forget one or two).

4

To break up a group (see Figure 4.24), choose Ungroup from the Object menu (Command-Shift-G)[Control-Shift-G].

Figure 4.24.

*Choosing Ungroup from
the Object menu.*

Groups can be nested, meaning you can have a group within a group, and so on. To better demonstrate the next tool, please select both the circles and the rectangles and group them. You'll now have one group of shapes that contains a group of rectangles and a group of circles.

The Group Selection Tool

The Group Selection tool is a variation of the Direct Selection tool (the white arrow) and can be found by pressing and holding the mouse button on the white arrow in the Toolbox. In complex illustrations, you may have nested groups that contain many groups. The Group Selection tool makes working with these files easy. To demonstrate, we'll be working in the same file as we did earlier with all the rectangles and circles.

1. Deselect everything (Command-Shift-A)[Control-Shift-A].
2. With the Group Selection tool, click one of the circles. Only the circle you clicked becomes selected.
3. Now click that same circle again. All of the circles are now selected.
4. Click that same circle *again*, and all of the rectangles become selected as well.

Each time you click with the Group Selection tool, it selects the next higher group, giving you easy access to any group within a nested group.

I promised earlier to tell you why the white arrow is so important in Illustrator. Switch back to the Direct Selection tool by selecting it from the Toolbox. Now press and hold down the (Option)[Alt] key. Notice that the Direct Selection tool has changed to the Group Selection tool. Releasing the (Option)[Alt] key returns you to the Direct Selection tool. Now you have the power to select parts of an object, or, simply by holding down the (Option)[Alt] key, you can select an entire object, or entire groups! For 90% of your work, you never have to go back to the black arrow.

4

Working with Selections

We can already see that selecting objects can become complicated. Now we will learn how Illustrator can help us out with selecting objects with certain settings and functions.

Area Select

We briefly mentioned Area Select in Hour 2, "Customizing Illustrator." In Illustrator's General Preferences, we had the option of activating Area Select, which makes selecting objects easier (by default, Area Select is turned on).

With Area Select turned on, you can select filled objects by clicking anywhere within the object. When Area Select is turned off, you must click an anchor point or the Bézier path of an object to select it (see Figure 4.25). An object filled with the None attribute is considered unfilled and can only be selected by clicking its Bézier path.

Figure 4.25.

The box on the left is being selected with Area Select activated, whereas the box on the right is being selected with Area Select deactivated.

Area Select only works in Preview mode. When in Artwork mode, you must click an object's Bézier path (or center point—see the following sidebar) to select it.

There is also another option called Type Area Select, which is covered in Hour 14, "Adding Text." Similar to Area Select, *Type* Area Select enables you to select type by clicking anywhere on the text.

Journey to the Center of the Vector

One of the characteristics of PostScript art is that each object has a center point. When you select an object, or view a page in Artwork mode, you can usually see an object's center point. Illustrator has the capability to show or hide the center point of any object via the Attributes palette (see Figure 4.26). Simply click the Don't Show Center or the Show Center button. When Snap-To-Point is turned on, using the center point of an object can be a big time saver and also make for easier alignment of objects.

Locking Objects

Illustrator gives you the ability to lock items. Locked items cannot be selected, moved, or edited until they are unlocked. This is an important feature for when files get complex, and you don't want to accidentally select objects you are not working on. There are also times when several objects are very close to each other (or even overlaying each other), and selecting the right one can be very difficult. By locking items that are not being edited, you can quickly select and edit the correct objects.

Figure 4.26.

By clicking the center point buttons, you can have Illustrator display or hide an object's center point.

Don't Show Center

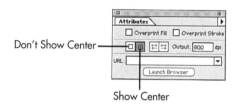

Show Center

To use the lock and unlock feature, select an object and then choose Lock (Command-L)[Control-L] from the Object menu (see Figure 4.27). You can lock several objects at a time, or you can keep locking items separately. To unlock all of your locked items, choose Unlock All (Command-Shift-L)[Control-Shift-L] from the Object menu.

Figure 4.27.

Choosing Lock from the Object menu.

Hiding Selections

If locking items won't do the trick, Illustrator also lets you hide objects from view. This has several uses. When working on one section of a complex file, hiding other parts makes it easier to concentrate on what you are working on, as well as make it easier for you to view what you are drawing onscreen. Even more importantly, hiding certain objects can give you a big speed boost. Placed images, objects filled with gradients or patterns, and other such items can severely slow down your screen redraw. If seeing those items is not critical to what you are working on, you can choose to hide those items, saving Illustrator from having to constantly redraw them.

To hide a selection, choose Hide Selection (Command-U)[Control-U] from the Object menu (see Figure 4.28). You can keep hiding objects as often as you like, individually or in groups, but when you choose Show All (Command-Shift-U)[Control-Shift-U] from the Object menu, all hidden objects become visible. There is no way to reveal only certain hidden objects.

Figure 4.28.

Hiding a selection by choosing Hide Selection from the Object menu.

Hide Edges

Those of you who have used Photoshop are probably familiar with this function. When you select an object, its path becomes highlighted in a color, and the object's anchor points become visible. This can sometimes interfere with viewing the object, and can make editing and creating artwork difficult, as well as annoying.

To hide a selected object's edges, choose Hide Edges (Command-H) from the View menu (see Figure 4.29). With edges turned off, you are not able to see which item is selected, so make sure you pay attention to what you click.

Figure 4.29.

Choosing the Hide Edges command from the View menu.

TIME SAVER

The Hide Edges command is a toggle, which means that it stays on until you turn it off by pressing (Command-H)[Control-H] again. Too many times, it's easy to forget that you turned edges off, and then you go crazy trying to figure out why nothing can be selected, when in reality, you just can't *see* that they're being selected.

4

Arranging Items

Although all drawn objects in Illustrator are on the same screen, they each appear in the order that they were drawn. In other words, if you were to draw two rectangles, one on top of another, the second rectangle would cover the first one and hide it from view. It's similar to having a stack of papers on your desk. If you want to shuffle the order of pages, you would take a paper from the bottom or middle of the pile and put it on top. Or you might take a paper from the top of the pile and move it to the bottom.

Illustrator gives you the ability to move objects all throughout the "pile." Under the Object menu you can find the Arrange submenu, which contains four commands (see Figure 4.30).

Figure 4.30.

The Arrange submenu.

☐ **Bring to Front**—brings the selected object to the front, similar to putting a paper on the top of the pile (see Figure 4.31).

☐ **Bring Forward**—brings the selected object forward one level, similar to moving a paper over the one directly above it (see Figure 4.32).

☐ **Send Backward**—sends the selected object one level backward, similar to putting a paper directly under the one it's resting on (see Figure 4.33).

☐ **Send to Back**—sends the selected object to the rear, similar to putting a paper on the bottom of the pile (see Figure 4.34).

When using groups, each group has its own set of levels. So if you bring an object that is part of a group to the front, it goes to the front of that group. In order to bring the object to the front of everything, you need to select the entire group and bring the whole group to the front.

Figure 4.31.

Starting out as the back-most object, the black square gets sent to the front with the Send to Front command.

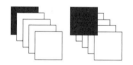

Figure 4.32.

The black square starts out as the rear-most object (left). After you apply Bring Forward, the black square moves forward one level (right).

Figure 4.33.

Here the black square begins as the topmost object (left), and is sent back one level using the Send Backward command (right).

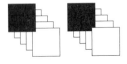

Figure 4.34.

Starting out as the topmost object (left), the black square gets sent to the back with the Send to Back command (right).

Summary

After learning all about selections and how they work, you should be feeling comfortable with moving things around, as well as know how to work with groups. You should also be able to lock and hide objects to make working easier. We also learned about arranging items and how objects are layered. In the next hour, we discuss Illustrator's layers, which is a powerful step above the kind of layering we just learned.

Term Review

Fill—The attribute that determines a color, gradient, or pattern for the interior of a shape.

Stroke—The attribute that determines the outline of an object.

Group—A collection of objects that all become selected when just one item in the group is selected.

Selection tool—The tool that looks like a black arrow; used to select entire objects.

Direct Selection tool—The tool that looks like a white arrow; used to select parts of an object.

Group Selection tool—The tool that looks like a white arrow with a plus sign next to it; used for selecting groups.

Marquee—A rectangular-shaped bounding box indicating an area to be selected.

Center point—A non-editable point that appears at the center of a vector object.

4

Hour 5

Working with Layers

In the last hour we covered moving objects to the front and to the back. We learned that each object was on its own level. Continuing on the topic of levels, it's time to learn about the king of all levels in Illustrator: *layers*. If you've worked in Photoshop, you're probably familiar with the concept of layers. If you'll forgive me for using the analogy, layers are similar to mechanical overlays. Clear sheets of acetate, these each contain parts of artwork, and when they are laid over each other, they form the complete art. Layers are extremely versatile and can really help keep complex illustrations under control and manageable. By viewing only certain layers, you can concentrate more easily on the task at hand. In this chapter, we learn all about these layers, including:

- ☐ The Layers palette
- ☐ Shuffling layers
- ☐ Hiding and locking layers
- ☐ Moving artwork between layers

The Layers Palette

Illustrator's layers are specified in the Layers palette. When you start a document, all artwork is automatically placed on a layer (see Figure 5.1). To open the Layers palette, choose Show Layers from the Window menu (see Figure 5.2).

Figure 5.1.
Illustrator's Layers palette.

Figure 5.2.
Choosing Show Layers from the Window menu.

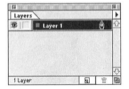

Editing Layers

There's a small controversy between designers as to when to create layers. Some artists prefer to create several layers before they begin working, adding the art to each layer as they progress. Others prefer to add or delete layers as necessary, as they work on a project. Still others like to create the entire piece, and then chop it up into different layers. No matter which way you do it, though, you have to learn how to add and discard layers.

Creating a New Layer

The easiest way to create a new layer is to click the New Layer button at the bottom of the Layers palette (see Figure 5.3). Illustrator creates the layer and assigns it a name. Don't worry, you won't have to keep your layers named "Layer 1" and "Layer 2." We'll change that when we learn about layer options later this hour.

Figure 5.3.
The New Layer button.

5

Another way to create a new layer is to select New Layer from the Layers palette menu (see Figure 5.4).

Figure 5.4.

Choosing New Layer from the Layers palette menu.

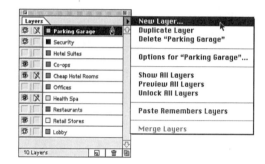

Deleting a Layer

To delete a layer, click the name of a layer and drag it to the Trash icon in the lower-right corner of the Layers palette (see Figure 5.5). Alternatively, you can delete a layer via the Layers palette menu. But what if the layer you are deleting contains artwork? Turns out Illustrator is keeping a watchful eye out for us. If you try to delete a layer with art on it, you get a warning message alerting you about the situation, and Illustrator only proceeds to delete the layer and its contents if you click OK. Otherwise Illustrator returns you to the document with the layer intact, where you can copy the art to another layer (see "Moving/Copying Items Between Layers" later in this hour).

Figure 5.5.

Deleting a layer with the Layers palette Trash icon.

Trash icon

Duplicating a Layer

Sometimes you want to make a copy of an entire layer. You can easily create a duplicate of a layer by clicking the name of an existing layer and dragging it to the New Layer icon on the bottom of the Layers palette (see Figure 5.6). Again, you can also create a duplicate by selecting Duplicate Layer from the Layers palette menu. The attributes, as well as all the artwork contained on that layer, are duplicated, and Illustrator adds the word "copy" to the layer name.

Figure 5.6.

Creating a duplicate layer by dragging an existing layer on top of the New Layer icon.

Create New Layer icon

Layer Options

Each layer has several attributes that facilitate your work, as well as add functionality to the layers. Double-clicking the name of a layer brings up the Layer Options dialog box (see Figure 5.7). Here you can name the layer, which is an important step. As you add more and more layers, it becomes increasingly difficult to remember which items are on Layer 23 and Layer 14. By giving intuitive names to layers (such as "Template," "Wheels," or "Ad Copy"), you can quickly identify where items are. In the Layer Options dialog box, you can also assign a selection color (see "Layer Colors," later in this hour), and choose to show, preview, or lock the layer (these are also discussed later in this chapter).

Figure 5.7.

Double-clicking the name of a layer brings up the Layer Options dialog box.

There are two more options found in the Layer Options dialog box: Print and Dim Images. By unchecking the Print box, you are telling Illustrator that you do not want the objects in this layer to print. You might want to create a layer where you write notes to yourself or a colleague, and putting it on a non-printing layer assures the text won't print when you send it to a client or for film separations. There also might be times when you have a complex illustration but only want to print specific parts of it.

TIME SAVER

In today's fast-paced world, a designer is sometimes forced to send a fax of a design to a client for instant approval. Fancy backgrounds and tints, however, can make text very difficult—if not impossible—to read when faxed. If you create your text and backgrounds on separate layers, you can use Layer Options to print only the text layer so that your client can read the clear text without the background. Just remember to set the background layer to print again before you send for final output.

5

The Dim Images button is used for when you want to use placed images as a template. Upon placing a bitmapped image, Illustrator dims the image to make it easier to trace over it. Try to avoid using this feature if possible, as it slows screen redraw. Of course, if you have no other choice, remember to turn the option off when you are done tracing. For more details on tracing images, see Hour 21, "Working Smart in Illustrator."

Layer Colors

If you have one or two layers in your document, it's pretty simple to keep track of which objects are on which layer. But in a document with many layers, it becomes increasingly difficult to remember which objects are on each layer. To make it easier to identify which object is on which layer, a color is defined for each layer. When an object is selected, it is highlighted in the color of its layer. When you create a new layer, Illustrator automatically assigns a new unique color to that layer. To change the color of a layer, simply double-click the layer to bring up the Layer Options dialog box, choose a new color (see Figure 5.8), and click OK.

Figure 5.8.

Choosing a new layer color.

Arranging Layers

What good would layers be if you couldn't shuffle the order of them around? By simply pressing and dragging on the layer name, you can change the order of the layers (see Figure 5.9). The order of layers determines which objects are in front of others. The objects of a layer closer to the top of the list in the Layers palette appear on top of those objects in layers closer to the bottom of the list.

Figure 5.9.

You can change the order of layers by simply dragging them.

5

Moving/Copying Items Between Layers

Many times you need to move objects from one layer to another. Instead of making you copy and paste objects, Illustrator has an intuitive feature built in to the Layers palette specifically for the purpose of moving and copying objects between layers.

When an object is selected, notice a little dot on the far right of the layer name in the Layers palette (see Figure 5.10). To move your selected object to another layer, simply click and drag the dot to another layer (see Figure 5.11), and the object is transferred to the new layer. The selection color changes to the new layer's color, too.

Figure 5.10.

The little dot on the far right indicates your selection.

Figure 5.11.

Dragging the dot to a different layer.

To copy objects to another layer, press and hold the (Option)[Alt] key as you drag the dot. A copy of your selection is put into the new layer.

Locking and Hiding Layers

One of the advantages of using layers is the ability to quickly lock or hide the objects on each layer. Notice that to the left of each layer are two boxes (see Figure 5.12). The left-hand box controls the view, whereas the right-hand box controls locking. An eye in the left box indicates that the layer is fully visible in your document.

Figure 5.12.

The visibility and lock boxes are on the far left of the Layers palette.

5

To hide the layer, click the eye, and the objects in that layer aren't visible in your document. Clicking again in the left box makes the layer visible. If you press and hold down the (Command)[Control] key while you click in the left-hand box, you set the layer to Artwork mode, as opposed to Preview mode. The little eye icon is hollow, indicating the change (see Figure 5.13). Simply (Command-click)[Control-click] again to return the layer to Preview mode.

Figure 5.13.

A hollow eye in the visibility box indicates the layer is in the Artwork view mode.

Click in the right-hand box and a pencil with a line through it appears indicating that the layer is locked (see Figure 5.14). Objects in a locked layer are visible in your document, but cannot be selected. To unlock the layer, click again in the right-hand box.

Figure 5.14.

In this document, layers Parking Garage, Cheap Hotel Rooms, and Health Spa are locked. Hotel Suites, Offices, and Restaurants are hidden, and Parking Garage, Security, and the Lobby layers are in Artwork mode.

It's important to remember that regardless of whether a layer is visible or locked, it prints unless you specify it as a non-printing layer in the Layer Options dialog box.

Summary

Layers are an important part of Illustrator, and we covered that in depth today. Although you may not use layers for simple illustrations, they can really come in handy as your illustrations become more complex. Speaking of complex, the next chapter introduces you to the most difficult part about Illustrator: the Pen tool and the Bézier curve—the heart of Illustrator.

5

Term Review

Layer color—Refers to the selection color of items on that layer (that is, if an object is selected, its anchor points appear in the color of that object's layer color).

Layer order—The stacking of layers upon each other. The layer order is determined by the position of each layer in the stack.

Hour 6

Drawing Bézier Paths

Strip away all of Illustrator's fancy features and new interface, and you're left with the heart of Illustrator—the *Bézier path* and the Pen tool. Since version 1.0, the Pen tool is probably the main reason why Illustrator has become one of today's best illustration programs. Comfortable, elegant, and functional, the Pen tool gives you complete control when creating and editing the base of all vector illustrations—the Bézier (pronounced BEH-zee-ay) path. In this hour, we discuss:

- ☐ The Bézier path
- ☐ Anchor points
- ☐ Drawing with the Pen tool

The Bézier Path

So what is a Bézier path anyway? It's a mathematical way of representing graphics, developed by Pierre Bézier (it was originally created to put designs of aircraft on a computer, and then later for designing cars). All vector objects are made up of Bézier path segments. Bézier paths come in two flavors, lines and curves. Let's discuss the difference between them.

The first type of Bézier path is a straight line and contains two *anchor points* with a straight line connecting them (see Figure 6.1). This is the simplest Bézier path and requires the least amount of memory to store and print. All that is needed is the coordinates of the first point and the second point.

Figure 6.1.

The simplest of Bézier paths: A straight line.

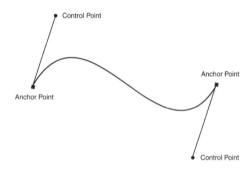

The second type of Bézier path is the curve, and here is where it gets complicated. A curve consists of two anchor points, with a curved line connecting them. The curve is determined by *control points*, which are attached to each anchor point (see Figure 6.2). The control points (also called handles) define exactly how the curved line is drawn between the two anchor points.

Figure 6.2.

A Bézier curve, showing the anchor points and the control points.

Of course, when the paths print, you won't see the anchor points or the handles. They are just there onscreen so that we can edit them, but when they print, all you see is the line (see Figure 6.3).

Figure 6.3.

When the files actually print, you don't see the anchor or the control points.

6

Up until now, we've been creating Bézier paths without even knowing it. The rectangles, ellipses, stars, polygons, and spirals that we've created are all made up of Bézier paths. We were doing fine until now, so why bring in all of this complicated anchor point and control point stuff? As they say, ignorance is bliss. Sure, you could do a lot of things in Illustrator without knowing what Bézier paths are. But you lose out on all the power that Illustrator offers. There are other programs out there that have more features than Illustrator. In fact, I think it would be safe to say that of all of the major illustration packages on the market, Illustrator has the *least* number of features. Illustrator's power lies within the Pen tool and the implementation of Bézier paths.

CAUTION

Before we begin learning how to create and edit Bézier paths and use the Pen tool, I want to make the following disclaimer:

Drawing and editing Bézier paths requires much patience and time. But you have a lot to look forward to—it also gets better with experience. I look back now at some of the art I created as a beginner, and I can't help but wonder, "What was I thinking?" There is no doubt that you will become comfortable with the Pen tool; you just have to give it time. Do the exercises listed here, *practice a lot,* and before you know it, you too will be looking back in wonder. But more importantly, you will have harnessed the power of the Pen tool.

The Pen Tool

Illustrator's Pen tool is rumored to be the most inhumane torture tool ever devised by man. But fear not, there is a method to the madness, and perseverance will prevail. The Pen tool is used to create precise Bézier paths of virtually any shape or form. It works by creating anchor points, which are the basis of Bézier paths.

JUST A MINUTE

Some of you who have used Photoshop know that there is a Pen tool in Photoshop as well, for defining clipping paths and precise selections. Both the Photoshop and the Illustrator Pen tool work identically, and you can even move Bézier paths between the two programs easily using cut and paste or drag and drop. It's integration such as this that really makes for intuitive, useful, and practical applications.

The Anchor Points

There are three different kinds of anchor points: the *straight corner point,* the *smooth point,* and the *combination point.* Each kind of anchor point has its specific attributes, and each is used to create different types of paths. A Bézier object can be made up of any of the three kinds of anchor points and can contain any combination as well. A square is made up of four straight corner anchor points, for example, whereas a circle is made up of four smooth anchor points. A shape such as a pie wedge contains both straight corner and smooth anchor points. As we go through the following hands-on exercises, you'll get a better feel for anchor points and understand how they work.

TIME SAVER

> Throughout this chapter, and the rest of the book, we will be doing different exercises in Illustrator. Although you can use this book without them, the files that I have used for Illustrations are available on the World Wide Web if you want to follow along. Simply direct your browser to `http://www.mordy.com`.

The Straight Corner Anchor Point

The straight corner is the simplest form of the anchor point, and it is used to define straight lines such as the ones shown previously in Figure 6.1. Before we begin using the Pen tool, it should be mentioned again that Illustrator's cursors change to indicate the current status of a tool. The subtle differences in the Pen tool cursor will be pointed out as they occur. If you goof anytime throughout the exercises, don't worry, just use the Undo command (Command-Z)[Control-Z].

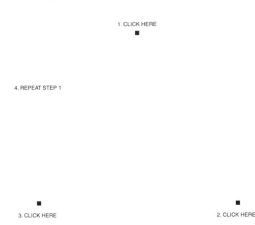

1. CLICK HERE

4. REPEAT STEP 1

3. CLICK HERE   2. CLICK HERE

6

1. Let's start by opening a new Illustrator document (Command-N)[Control-N].

2. Select the Pen tool from the Toolbox (see Figure 6.4). Notice that the Pen tool cursor has a small "x" on the lower right (see Figure 6.5). This indicates you are starting a new path.

Figure 6.4.

Selecting Illustrator's Pen tool.

Figure 6.5.

The tell-tale cursor. The little "x" indicates the Pen tool is ready to create a new path.

3. Let's create a triangle. Click once. Click again to the lower right, and again to the left (see Figure 6.6). Notice that the cursor has now changed to a plain Pen tool, indicating that you are in the midst of creating a shape.

Figure 6.6.

Two segments of the triangle, completed.

4. Now drag your cursor up to the first point you created. Notice that when the cursor touches the point, a little "o" appears on the lower right of the Pen tool cursor (see Figure 6.7). This indicates that you are about to close, or complete, a path.

6

Figure 6.7.

By showing the little "o", the Pen tool is indicating that clicking will complete and close the path.

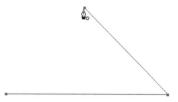

5. Click the top anchor point to complete the triangle. The Pen tool cursor appears
   with the "x" again, ready to start a new path (see Figure 6.8).

Figure 6.8.

After completing the triangle, the Pen tool is ready for its next assignment.

Congratulations! You have just created your first shape with the Pen tool. Don't jump for joy just yet, the hard part comes next: The smooth anchor point.

The Smooth Anchor Point

The smooth anchor point contains two control points, or handles. By adjusting the control points, you determine the slope and sharpness of the curve on either side of the point. Because the path continues through the point without a sharp change in direction, it is called a smooth anchor point.

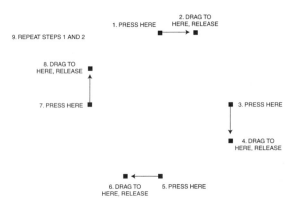

1. Using the Pen tool, press and drag a point to the right, about half an inch. Notice that when you drag, you are pulling a control point out from the anchor point (see Figure 6.9).

Figure 6.9.

When you press the mouse button, you define where the anchor point is. By dragging, you define where the control point is.

6

2. Release the mouse button.

3. Move your cursor about one inch down and to the right of the first anchor point—*not the control point* (see Figure 6.10).

Figure 6.10.
Without clicking, you move your cursor to where the next anchor point will be.

4. Press and drag down about half an inch (see Figure 6.11).

Figure 6.11.
While still holding down the mouse button, drag as shown.

5. Release the mouse button. You should now see the first arc of a circle.

6. Move your cursor one inch down and to the *left* of the last *anchor point* you created (see Figure 6.12).

Figure 6.12.
Repositioning the cursor for the next step.

7. Press and drag to the left about half an inch (see Figure 6.13).

8. Release the mouse button. We're halfway there!

9. Move your cursor one inch *up* and to the left of the anchor point you just created (see Figure 6.14).

Figure 6.13.

Dragging out another control point.

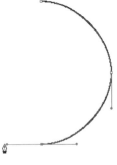

Figure 6.14.

This is the last anchor point, bringing the total anchor points in this shape to four.

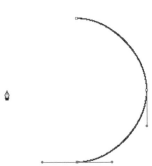

10. Press and drag up about half an inch (see Figure 6.15).

Figure 6.15.

Dragging out another control point.

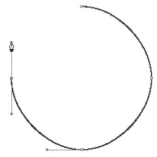

11. Release the mouse button.

12. To complete the circle, repeat Step 1—click the *first anchor point* we created and drag about half an inch to the right (see Figure 6.16).

6

Figure 6.16.

Completing the circle.

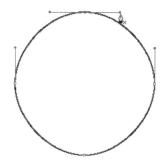

13. Release the mouse button, and voilà! a circle!

So we see that by pressing and dragging a point, we can create a smooth anchor point with control handles. Control handles determine the direction of the curved path. To demonstrate, switch to the Direct Selection tool (the white arrow) and click the line of the circle. The control points are now visible for that section of the path. Press and drag on one of the control handles, and see how the path behaves when you move the control point.

Generally, the direction of the curve follows the control point. Try to avoid stretching the handles too far from the anchor point as it makes for difficult editing (the ideal guideline shouldn't exceed one third the length of the curve). Again, as you work more and more with control points, you get a better idea of where to place them and how to achieve the curve you want.

The Combination Anchor Point

Okay, we're building confidence now, and we're really going to need it. The *Combination Point* is—get this—a combination of the straight anchor point and the smooth anchor point, and things can get a bit confusing.

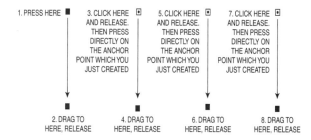

1. Let's begin by pressing and dragging a point down about one inch. Release the mouse button (see Figure 6.17).

2. Position your cursor one inch to the right of the first anchor point.

Figure 6.17.

Dragging the first point.

3. Click the mouse (see Figure 6.18).

Figure 6.18.

*A single click completes
the path—the first
anchor point was a
smooth point, the second
a straight point.*

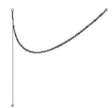

4. Position your cursor directly atop the anchor point you just created. Notice that the pen cursor changes to show a small inverted "V" on the lower right (see Figure 6.19).

Figure 6.19.

*Notice the change in the
Pen tool cursor.*

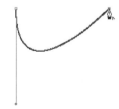

5. Click the point, and drag down one inch (holding the Shift key while you drag keeps it a straight line).
6. Repeat Steps 2 through 5 (see Figure 6.20).

6

Figure 6.20.
Making waves.

In the above exercise, you create a straight anchor point, which has no control handles, when you click. By dragging out of the straight point, you are defining the *next connecting* path and anchor point. So, in reality, the *combination point* has two sides to it: a straight side (from the single click) and a curved side (from the click and drag).

True, in these examples, you were told where to place the anchor points and the control points. If you were creating any other random shape, you would have to decide where those points belong on your own. After getting a feel for how anchor points and control points affect the path, you will be able to make these decisions on your own. I've included several other templates, shown here, that you can use to get a better feel for the Pen tool.

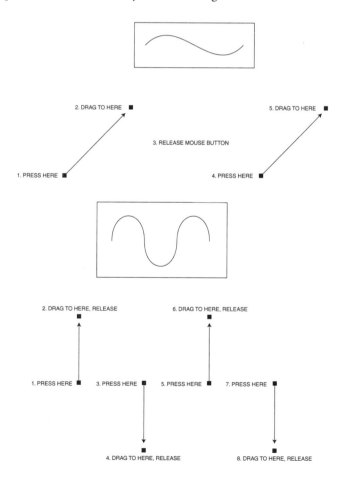

6

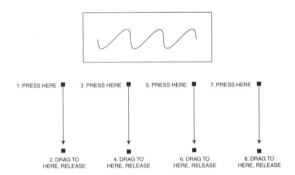

Open and Closed Paths

A path in Illustrator can either be open or closed. An open path has two endpoints, whereas a closed path has none—one end joins the other. As you draw with the Pen tool, Illustrator uses the current fill and stroke attributes for your shape. As you complete each click, Illustrator attempts to fill the shape using the current fill, so do not be alarmed. Just continue following the steps in the exercise. We cover fills and strokes in detail in Hours 10 and 11.

Summary

Whew! This was the hardest chapter yet. Give yourself a big hand for making it through the horrors of the Pen tool. But don't worry, it will become second nature before you know it. We also learned about Bézier paths and the different kinds of anchor points. Next we work with Bézier paths after we've created them. This is going to be *fun!*

Term Review

Bézier path—A mathematically defined line consisting of *anchor points* and *control points.*

Open path—A Bézier path with two open (unconnected) endpoints.

Closed path—A Bézier path that is fully enclosed; it has no beginning and no end.

Anchor point—A defined point on a Bézier path.

Control point—A defined point that is part of an anchor point, used to control the curve of a path.

Smooth point—An anchor point in which its control points are tangent to the anchor point.

Corner point—An anchor point with no control points; for defining straight lines.

Combination point—An anchor point that shares the attributes of both a smooth point and a corner point.

6

Hour 7

Editing Bézier Paths

No one is perfect, and there are always times when you need to edit a path to get it just right. There are also plenty of times when you create a simple path and modify it to create a more complex path. Perhaps the greatest advantage a computer offers is the ability to easily make changes over and over again. In Illustrator, editing a path can be done in several ways, and this hour we discuss these issues, including:

- ☐ Adding and deleting anchor points
- ☐ Using the Reshape tool
- ☐ Cutting paths
- ☐ Joining paths

Manipulating Existing Points

After you draw a path, you might want to change the shape or style of the points, adjusting the curve of the path or making a corner point a smooth point. There are several tools that enable you to modify a path by changing, adding, or deleting points.

The Direct Selection Tool

Perhaps the simplest form of editing a path is with the white arrow, or Direct Selection tool. By selecting only one anchor point you can reposition it. By selecting a path and then dragging on a control point you can change the shape of the curve (see Figure 7.1).

Figure 7.1.

Editing a path's curve by dragging the control point with the Direct Selection tool.

TIME SAVER

The P key is the keyboard shortcut for the Pen tool. Pressing it repeatedly cycles through the Pen tool, the Add Anchor Point tool, the Delete Anchor Point tool, and the Convert Direction Point tool.

The Add Anchor Point Tool

Simple in concept, the Add Anchor Point tool enables you to put additional anchor points on an existing path (see Figure 7.2). The new point takes on the attributes of the path that you click (see Figure 7.3). If you add a point to a straight path, the new anchor point is a straight anchor point, and clicking a curved path results in a new smooth anchor point.

Figure 7.2.

Selecting the Add Anchor Point tool.

Figure 7.3.

A point added to a straight path, and a curved one.

The Delete Anchor Point Tool

The Delete Anchor Point tool, shown in Figure 7.4, simply deletes existing points. By clicking an anchor point with the Delete Anchor Point tool, the point is removed, and Illustrator automatically joins the preceding anchor point with the next point on the path (see Figure 7.5).

7

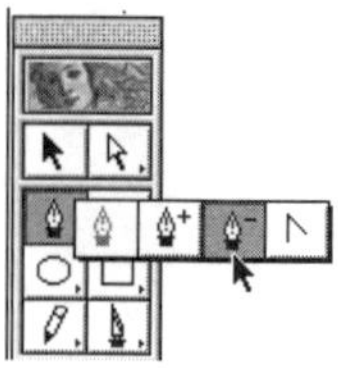

Figure 7.4.
*Selecting the Delete
Anchor Point tool.*

Figure 7.5.
*A square before (left) and
after (right) using the
Delete Anchor Point tool
to delete the lower-right
point.*

The Convert Direction Point Tool

What do you do when you already have an anchor point but you need to change it from one
type of point to another? You use the Convert Direction Point tool. The last tool from the
pen tool quartet, the Convert Direction Point tool, shown in Figure 7.6, can easily be accessed
by pressing (Command-Option)[Control-Alt] when the Direct Selection tool is active.
Notice the cursor changes to an inverted "V" shape (see Figure 7.7).

Figure 7.6.
*Selecting the Convert
Direction Point tool.*

Figure 7.7.
*The inverted "V" shape
indicating the Convert
Direction Point tool is
in use.*

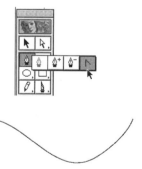

Working in the same way the Pen tool does, clicking a point converts it to a straight anchor
point. Pressing and dragging on a point makes that point a smooth anchor point. In order
to make a smooth point into a combination point, press and drag on a control point (see
Figure 7.8). If you want to convert a straight anchor point to a combination point, you must
first make the point a smooth point, then press and drag on the control point.

7

Figure 7.8.

Creating a combination point with the Convert Direction Point tool.

Editing Paths

Illustrator 7 offers several tools for controlling and editing paths. The newest, the Reshape tool, modifies the shape of a curve without requiring you to select a control point. The Knife and Scissors tools cut paths, whereas the Join and Average commands connect paths together.

The Reshape Tool

One of the new features of Illustrator 7 is the Reshape tool (see Figure 7.9). By simply clicking and dragging a path, you can reshape a curved path without having to select a control point. Even more important, the Reshape tool has the capability to edit multiple control points at the same time (see Figure 7.10). In contrast, the Direction Selection tool can only edit one control point at a time.

Figure 7.9.

Selecting Illustrator's new Reshape tool.

Figure 7.10.

The first star is the original. The second star has been scaled, but notice it was only stretched at one point in the object. The third star was scaled with the Reshape tool. Notice how the scale has been applied evenly throughout the selected points.

The Reshape tool can also quickly add points to a path to increase the editabilty of the path. When you move the Reshape tool over a part of the path where no point exists, the cursor changes to indicate that a point can go there (see Figure 7.11). Simply clicking or pressing and dragging places the point.

7

Figure 7.11.

Notice the change in the cursor as it approaches the line.

The Scissors Tool

Sometimes editing a path calls for splitting it in two. The Scissors tool, shown in Figure 7.12, is used to sever an individual path. With the Scissors tool selected, you can click anywhere on any path and Illustrator severs the path where you clicked. A path need not even be selected when using the Scissors tool, so be careful where you click when using it.

Figure 7.12.

The Scissors tool.

The Scissors tool can be quite a pain to use, as you have to click exactly on the path you want to cut. Also, in most cases, you are using the Scissors tool to cut a line and join it to another, which just means more editing. If all the clicking and joining frustrates you (as it does me), then stick around when we get to Hour 13, "The Pathfinder Commands," where we learn about some cool path editing commands. You'll never use the Scissors tool again...

The Knife Tool

Based on the same premise of the Scissors tool, the Knife tool is used to sever objects (see Figure 7.13). The similarities end there, however. To use the Knife tool, drag it over an object, and the object is sliced where you dragged, just as if you had cut it with a knife, leaving you two (or more) filled objects (see Figure 7.14).

Figure 7.13.

Selecting the Knife tool.

Figure 7.14.

Slicing an object with the Knife tool.

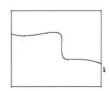

7

An important thing to remember here is that the Knife tool cuts through all objects that cross its path, even unselected ones. So dragging the Knife tool over a group of items slices all of the items (see Figure 7.15). This is a great feature that has a lot of uses, but there are also times when you only want to cut through one selected object without cutting what is underneath. To do so, hold down the Shift key before pressing and dragging, and Illustrator only slices the selected object (see Figure 7.16). Holding the Shift key also constrains the Knife tool to slice in straight lines only.

Figure 7.15.
The Knife tool slices all objects it crosses, even those layered underneath.

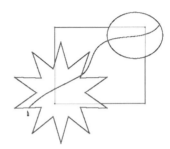

Figure 7.16.
Using the Shift key, you can slice just selected objects.

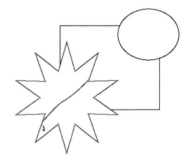

TIME SAVER

After you start dragging with the Shift key down, you can release the Shift key and draw a freeform path, and Illustrator still only slices the selected object. You can also slice multiple objects in straight lines by first pressing and dragging with the Knife tool *and then* pressing the Shift key.

The Join and Average Commands

Alas, there will come a time when you want to connect one path with another. Say you have a square, for example, but only three sides have lines between the points. You need to connect the last two points to complete the square. It's easy with the Join command. Found by choosing Object➡Path➡Join, Join does one of three things:

☐ Close an open path if the entire path is selected (see Figure 7.17).

7

☐ Connect two separate points with a line, be it the endpoints of a single path, or the endpoints of two different paths (see Figure 7.18).

☐ Connect two overlapping points by combining them into one point (see Figure 7.19).

Figure 7.17.

Quickly closing an open path with the Join command.

Figure 7.18.

Connecting the dots. You can clean up the resulting path with the Delete Anchor Point tool.

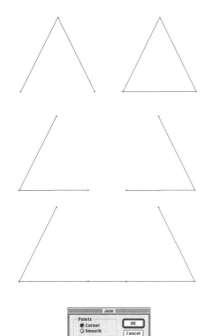

Figure 7.19.

When joining two overlapping points, Illustrator asks if you want to make the new combined point a smooth or corner anchor point.

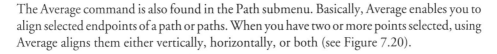

The Average command is also found in the Path submenu. Basically, Average enables you to align selected endpoints of a path or paths. When you have two or more points selected, using Average aligns them either vertically, horizontally, or both (see Figure 7.20).

Figure 7.20.

From left to right: original lines with the left endpoints selected, then averaged horizontally, vertically, and both.

7

Drawing Paths with the Freehand Tool

Now that you've learned all about the Pen tool, there's a much easier way to draw a Bézier path. The Freehand tool, shown in Figure 7.21, and no relation to the rival program FreeHand, lets you click and drag on the screen, and Illustrator places the anchor points for you (see Figure 7.22). So why bother with the Pen tool? Because it's very difficult to create precise drawings with the Freehand tool. It's great for say, signing your name, or making quick sketch lines, but for most of your work, the Pen tool is better. Besides, after creating a path with the Freehand tool, you may still have to "clean it up" by editing the path. Now that you can edit anchor points and handles, it's easy to work on any path, no matter how it was created.

Figure 7.21.

Illustrator's Freehand tool.

Figure 7.22.

You just draw, Illustrator does the rest.

Drawing with the mouse (or even a tablet) is not anything like drawing with a pencil, and it takes time to get comfortable with the way a mouse or tablet stylus feels. To make life a bit easier, you can control how sensitive Illustrator's Freehand tool is by changing the setting in the Curve Fitting Tolerance box found in General Preferences (see Figure 7.23). As I mentioned in Hour 2, "Customizing Illustrator," you can use a setting anywhere from 1 to 10, 1 being the most sensitive to every move, and 10 being the least sensitive, making for smoother lines.

Figure 7.23.

Setting the Curve Fitting Tolerance in Preferences.

7

Time Saver

Holding down the (Command)[Control] key while dragging with the Freehand tool changes your cursor to an eraser that you can use to quickly delete parts of your path while still drawing with it (see Figure 7.24). Illustrator only erases the path in the reverse order in which you drew it, and you cannot erase a portion from the middle of your path.

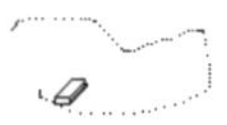

Figure 7.24.

Using the eraser to delete parts of a line as you draw.

Summary

We now know the different ways you can edit Bézier paths in Illustrator, and we learned how to modify paths by cutting them with the Scissors and Knife tools and also by joining and averaging them. We also learned how to use the Freehand tool. You're doing great, and in the next hour we explore compound paths and masking techniques.

7

Hour 8

Compound Paths and Masks

Until now, we have dealt with single objects in Illustrator—a square, a circle, a star, even a set of waves. Now, we begin to utilize several objects together. I am not referring to the kind of groups we covered back in Hour 4, "Working with Selections." Each of the concepts covered in this chapter use more than one object to create what looks like just one object, such as:

- ☐ Compound paths
- ☐ Masking objects
- ☐ Masking placed images

Compound Paths

Let's think back to our chemistry days. Remember what a compound is? It's a substance made up of a mixture of two or more elements. Similarly, a *compound path* is a path made up of two or more paths. So you're probably wondering, how is that different from making a group? Well, a group is just a bunch of objects all thrown together, but each object is separate by itself. In a compound path, all the paths included are considered to be one path. You can't fill each shape with a different color—the entire compound path can only have one fill and stroke attribute.

So what are compound paths used for? For making objects with holes "cut out" of them, such as the letter "O" (see Figure 8.1).

Figure 8.1.

As a compound path (left) you can see through the letter "O," but if the "O" is two paths, just a black circle with a white one on top, you can't see what is behind the "O."

Now let's create our own compound path:

1. Draw a nice-sized rectangle.
2. Draw a circle within the rectangle.
3. Select both objects.
4. Press (Command-8)[Control-8], or choose Object→Compound Paths→Make (see Figure 8.2).

Figure 8.2.

Choosing Make Compound Paths.

8

You can release a compound path by pressing (Command-Option-8)[Control-Alt-8] or by choosing Object→Compound Paths→Release.

So now I know how to create a compound path, but how does it *work?*

It's All in the Direction

The most significant and unique aspect of a compound path is the ability to *change the direction* of a path within the compound. All shapes travel in one direction, either clockwise or counter-clockwise (see Figure 8.3). In a compound path, paths can run *both* clockwise and counter-clockwise.

Figure 8.3.

The arrows indicate the direction of each path.

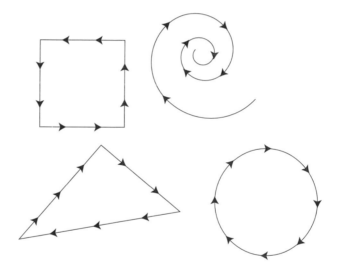

Let's look at the "O" again. Notice that the direction of the inner path is going in the opposite direction of the outer path (see Figure 8.4). How does this give the "O" a hollow center? Well, imagine you had a pair of scissors, and you had to cut out the letter "O." How would you cut it out using only one cut, not two? You'd cut around the outside of the "O" then slice through the "O," and cut the inside out (see Figure 8.5). Notice that when you're cutting the inside, you're going in the opposite direction than you were when you were cutting the outside. Although you can't see where the slice is, in reality, that's what Illustrator is doing.

Figure 8.4.

The inner path is going clockwise, whereas the outer path is going counter-clockwise.

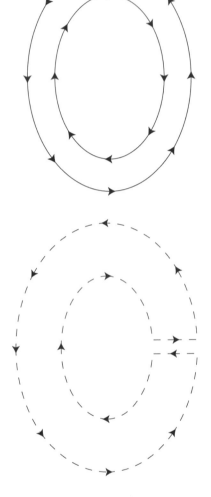

Figure 8.5.

As you trace around the shape, the direction changes as you move to the inside.

There might be times when you need to change the direction of a path in a compound path (especially when you have more than two paths) in order to make the path hollow. In the Attributes palette (Command-Shift-I)[Control-Shift-I] are the Reverse Path Direction buttons (see Figure 8.6). They are only active when a compound path is selected. Click either button to reverse the path to make a shape hollow.

Figure 8.6.

*The Reverse Path
Direction buttons in the
Attributes palette.*

8

Masks

What's a mask? Just like a mask covers part of your face, a mask in Illustrator covers part of your artwork. Say you have this photo of your graduating class, for example, and you want to just show the part with you and your best friend, who is standing next to you. By drawing a square and making it a mask, you can have only the parts of the photo that are behind the square be visible. The rest of the photo does not show.

For this next exercise, I created a *beautiful* file, called shapes, that contains many circles and squares (see Figure 8.7). You can either try and duplicate this file, or create one of your own (If you create your own file, make sure to group all of the art when you are done).

Figure 8.7.

My shapes.

1. With the file open, draw a new shape, about half the size of the artwork. I've chosen to use a star (see Figure 8.8). Notice the shape blocks out a good portion of our artwork because it is in front. A mask must always be in front of the artwork.

Figure 8.8.

The star will be our mask.

2. Select everything by pressing (Command-A)[Control-A] (see Figure 8.9).

Figure 8.9.

Everything selected.

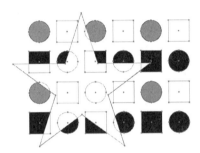

3. Choose Object➥Masks➥Make (see Figure 8.10). Deselect all by pressing (Command-Shift-A)[Control-Shift-A].

Figure 8.10.

Making the mask.

You just created a mask! Now you can only see the artwork that is within the mask, and the rest is hidden (see Figure 8.11). But don't worry, the rest of the artwork is still there. In fact, one of the greatest things about Illustrator's Mask feature is that you can move the artwork within the mask. Let's try it!

Figure 8.11.

The masked artwork.

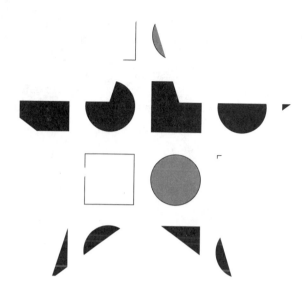

1. Choose the Selection tool (black arrow).

2. Click one of the circles or squares. Because the artwork is grouped, it all becomes selected, except for the mask of course.

3. Move the artwork about an inch to the left.

Of course you can even edit the artwork, and the mask will still be in effect. To remove the mask, select it and choose Object→Mask→Release (see Figure 8.12). So a mask is just like a window where you can place different images behind it and move them around for quick and easy editing and positioning. Masking is also great with placed images and with type, which we get to in later chapters.

Figure 8.12.

Releasing a mask.

Summary

This hour covered two very important concepts: compound paths, which basically enable us to cut holes through the middle of objects, and what a mask is and how we can use masks to control what parts of an image or what parts of objects are visible. Are you ready for a little splash of color? Better get your smock ready for the next hour!

Hour **9**

Coloring Objects

Well, all these shapes in black and white are nice, but let's move out of the dark ages, and start our own renaissance. Let's add some color! Illustrator has lots of options when it comes to coloring objects. Besides solid colors, Illustrator can fill objects with gradients and patterns—all customizable. Illustrator also has support for custom colors such as Pantone, TRUMATCH, and even web-specific colors (for use on the World Wide Web). Throughout this chapter we discuss each of these in detail, including:

- ☐ The Color palette
- ☐ The Swatches palette
- ☐ The Eyedropper tool
- ☐ The Paint Bucket tool

Fill and Stroke

In Illustrator, each object has two attributes: a *fill* and a *stroke* (see Figure 9.1). As we'll soon see, Illustrator has several kinds of fills and strokes. You can give a fill and a stroke to just about any object (with the exception of a mask), even one that is an open path (see Figure 9.2).

Figure 9.1.

Each object has a fill and a stroke.

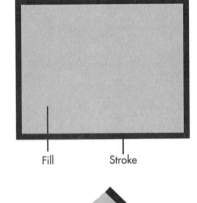

Fill   Stroke

Figure 9.2.

Illustrator fills an open path by using the two open points as a boundary.

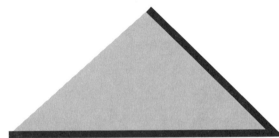

At the bottom of the Toolbox are the Fill and Stroke indicators (see Figure 9.3). These are very similar to Photoshop's Foreground and Background color indicators. The box to the upper left is the Fill indicator, and the one to the lower right is the Stroke indicator. You can click either one to make it active, or you can press X to toggle between them. When the Fill box is selected, any changes you make in the Color palette are applied to the fill of a selected object, and the same is true for the Stroke.

Figure 9.3.

Illustrator's Fill and Stroke indicators.

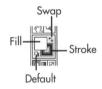

Swap

Fill——   ——Stroke

Default

There are two more icons there: One with little arrows to the upper right, and one with little boxes to the lower right. Clicking the arrows swaps the fill and stroke, meaning if the fill is currently white and the stroke is black, clicking the arrow makes the fill black and the stroke white. Clicking the little boxes sets the fill and stroke to Illustrator's default setting (as does pressing D), which is a white fill and black stroke. Note that this does not affect the weight (thickness) of the stroke.

JUST A MINUTE

When changing the color of the fill or stroke, any object that is selected while you make the change will take on the new color attributes. If no object is selected, the next object you create will take on the new color attributes you just set.

The Color Palette

Illustrator's Color palette, shown in Figure 9.4, consists of a single large swatch, a color slider (or sliders) with percentage boxes, and a color bar, which, depending on what colors are selected, is either a color spectrum or a grayscale/tint ramp. If all you see is the color bar, select Show Options from the palette menu (see Figure 9.5).

Figure 9.4.

Illustrator's Color palette.

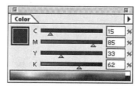

Figure 9.5.

Selecting Show Options in the Color palette.

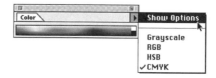

Illustrator works with any of four different *color models*: CMYK, grayscale, RGB, and HSB. To quickly cycle through each of the color models, hold down the Shift key, and click the big swatch in the Color palette (see Figure 9.6).

Figure 9.6.

Shift-clicking the swatch in the Color palette cycles through each of Illustrator's four color models.

Selecting a Color

To select a color, either click anywhere in the color spectrum or tint ramp, or adjust the sliders manually by clicking on the little triangles and dragging them to the left and right. You can also enter percentages manually by clicking in the field, entering a number, and pressing the Tab key to advance to the next field, or Shift-Tab to go back to the previous field.

TIME SAVER

After you put the "focus" into the color palette, you can quickly move through all the fields by pressing the Tab key. If you have other palettes docked to it as well, such as the Gradient or Stroke palette, you can cycle through those fields as well. To put Illustrator's focus into the last used palette, press (Command-~)[Control-~].

TIME SAVER

Illustrator's slider bars are very intuitive and change color as you drag to approximate other colors. You can also hold down the Shift key while dragging any one slider and all sliders move proportionately, making it easy to get lighter or darker shades of process colors.

Color Models

I mentioned that Illustrator supports four different color models. Illustrator also enables you to have colors from different color models within the same document (see the following Note). It's important to keep this in mind as you work on each project. Some jobs may require that you work in CMYK, others in RGB, and so on. In order to assure that your finished artwork looks as you intended it to be, make sure you are using the right color model from the beginning. Switching between color models after a job is in progress or finished may result in color shifts and changes.

JUST A MINUTE

Although Illustrator lets you have a document containing colors from different color models, that doesn't mean you should do it. In fact, it can be very bad. If you are working on a job that will be printed, use *only* the CMYK or Grayscale color model. If you are doing multimedia work, use RGB or HSB. Using different color models within the same document can make for non-consistent color shifts and can become a production nightmare.

CMYK

The *CMYK* color model (cyan, magenta, yellow, and black) is the standard for most of today's offset printing and is also known as four-color process. If your color artwork will be printed on paper, you're most probably going to create it in CMYK. To select a CMYK color from the Color palette, either Shift-click to cycle through the color models until CMYK shows up, or choose CMYK from the palette menu (see Figure 9.7).

Figure 9.7.
Choosing the CMYK color model.

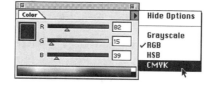

Grayscale

For black and white work, use *grayscale*, which supports 256 levels of gray. You have the ability to create different percentages of black. In this mode, the Color palette has a grayscale ramp to choose different percentages (see Figure 9.8).

Figure 9.8.
The grayscale ramp in the Color palette.

RGB

The *RGB* color model (red, green, and blue) is the standard used for today's televisions and computer monitors. If you are designing work for multimedia applications or for the World Wide Web, use the RGB color palette. RGB colors have a much wider range, or *gamut*, and have more colors that are brighter than CMYK. For more information on web colors, see Hour 23, "Web Graphics."

HSB

The *HSB* color model (hue, saturation, and brightness) is not as widely used and is based upon the human perception of color. The hue value determines which color you get, while saturation determines how intense that color is, and brightness determines how light or dark it is. In most cases, though, if you are using HSB colors, you will eventually have to convert them to RGB or CMYK for output.

Custom Colors

Though not a color model, there is another kind of color supported within Illustrator: custom colors. A *custom color* is a predefined color that you can either create or choose from a list such as Pantone, Focoltone, TOYO, or TRUMATCH. Custom colors are also called *spot colors*. These are standard colors that have been designated to assure color accuracy.

The Pantone system, for example, was created so that when a designer wanted to print red, he could specify a Pantone number, which a printer could match exactly by using a red ink, instead of producing the color with a combination of cyan, magenta, yellow, and black inks. Custom colors act the same way as grayscale does. You can specify a tint of a custom color, and the Color palette looks identical.

Loading Custom Color Palettes

Included with Illustrator are several useful custom color libraries. These include DICCOLOR, FOCOLTONE, PANTONE (coated, process, and uncoated), TOYO, and TRUMATCH, plus system palettes for both Macintosh and Windows for multimedia work. Illustrator also has a wonderful color-safe web palette for use when creating art for the World Wide Web.

To load any of these palettes, choose Swatch Libraries from the Window menu (see Figure 9.9), and choose one of the libraries. But let's say you went through all the trouble of creating your own custom colors in one document, and you want to use them in another one. That's when you select Other Library from the submenu (see Figure 9.10), after which Illustrator asks you to locate another Illustrator file, and imports its custom colors.

Figure 9.9.

Choosing a custom color library.

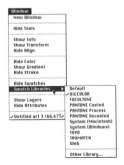

Figure 9.10.

Importing custom colors from another Illustrator file.

The Swatches Palette

Imagine if every time you wanted to apply a color, you had to enter the percentages of that color in the Color palette. Besides being a pain, it would also be a big waste of time. That's where the Swatches palette comes in. A *swatch* is a color that you define. It can be a process color, a spot color, or even a gradient or pattern, as we'll soon see. After you define a swatch, you can apply it to any object. You can also edit and modify an existing swatch.

Let's take a look at the Swatches palette (see Figure 9.11). If the palette is not already open, press F5 to open it, or choose Show Swatches from the Window menu.

Figure 9.11.

The Swatches palette.

First, notice the little "chicklet" icons across the bottom of the palette. From the left, the first one is Show All Swatches. The next three are for Color, Gradient, and Pattern swatches, respectively. At first glance, the palette may look too messy, and it may be difficult to determine what's what. By clicking the color, gradient, or pattern icons, you can choose to view only those swatches, making it easier to choose a swatch (see Figure 9.12).

Figure 9.12.

The chicklet icons on the bottom of the Swatches palette. Notice that only the gradient swatches are shown.

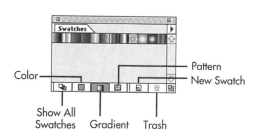

Next are the New Swatch and Trash icons. Clicking the New Swatch icon creates a new swatch with whatever color is currently selected. (Selected swatches have a white border.) Clicking the Trash icon deletes any selected swatch. To select a swatch, simply click it. You can select several contiguous swatches by holding down the Shift key, or you can select non-contiguous swatches by holding the (Command)[Control] key when selecting the swatches (see Figure 9.13).

Figure 9.13.

Selecting multiple swatches with the (Command)[Control] key.

TIME SAVER

Illustrator has drag-and-drop capabilities. You can delete swatches by dragging them into the Trash icon, and you can also create a duplicate swatch by dragging an existing swatch on top of the New Swatch icon. You can drag colors between the Fill and Stroke indicators, the Color palette, and even between custom color and Swatches palettes!

Double-clicking a swatch brings up the Swatch Options dialog box (see Figure 9.14). You can then edit the name of the swatch, as well as determine whether it should be a spot or process color. If you want to change the values of an existing swatch, follow these steps:

Figure 9.14.

The Swatch Options dialog box.

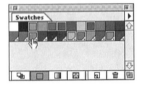

1. Select the swatch you want to modify.

2. In the Color palette, edit the color.

3. When you're done editing the color, click and drag the color swatch.

4. While still pressing the mouse, hold down the (Option)[Alt] key, and drag the color swatch (either the one in the Colors palette or the one in the Toolbox) on top of the swatch you want to edit in the Swatches palette.

You'll notice that some swatches have a small dot in the lower-right corner. The dot indicates that the swatch is a spot color. You can also change the order of the swatches simply by dragging and moving them around.

Viewing the Swatches Palette

Illustrator also gives you three ways to view the Swatches palette: Name, Small Swatch, or Large Swatch (see Figure 9.15). To choose a viewing mode, select a choice from the palette menu. You can also select the functions we've mentioned earlier, such as Duplicate Swatch and Delete Swatch, as well as sort the swatches by kind or name (see Figure 9.16). When you view swatches by name, an icon on the far right of the swatch name indicates whether the swatch is spot or process.

Figure 9.15.

The three viewing modes of the Swatches palette.

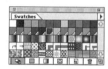 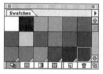 

Figure 9.16.

Sorting the swatches through the palette menu.

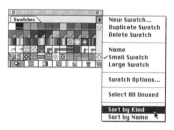

TIME SAVER

Although there is no swatch in the Swatches palette for the None attribute, remember that there is a keyboard shortcut for it. To quickly fill an object or stroke it with None, press the slash (/) key. Whether the fill or stroke of the selected object is changed to None depends on the focus of the Fill and Stroke icons on the Toolbox.

TIME SAVER

After you put the focus into the Swatches palette (Command-~)[Control-~], you can type the first few letters of a color, or the numbers of a Pantone color, and Illustrator jumps to that swatch. Press Enter to bring the focus back into your artwork.

The Eyedropper Tool

The Eyedropper tool, as shown in Figure 9.17, is used to sample colors for use in applying those colors and attributes to other objects. Say you have a shape with one color, for example, and you want it to be the color of another shape. Without deselecting your shape, you can switch to the Eyedropper tool and click the other object. This colors your selected object to be the same as the one you double-clicked on.

Figure 9.17.

The Eyedropper tool.

You can also press and hold down the mouse while using the Eyedropper tool, and then drag *anywhere* to sample the pixel color of *anything* on your screen (in real time, I might add— it's cool to watch the colors zip through the Fill indicator).

To control exactly which attributes the Eyedropper (and Paint Bucket) picks up, double-click the Eyedropper tool in the Toolbox. Illustrator presents you with a comprehensive dialog box where you can specify settings for picking up strokes and fills (see Figure 9.18).

Figure 9.18.

Specifying options for the Eyedropper and Paint Bucket tools.

The Paint Bucket Tool

Working in tandem with the Eyedropper tool, the Paint Bucket tool, as shown in Figure 9.19, applies colors to unselected objects. You just click an object and Illustrator fills that object with whatever color is selected.

Figure 9.19.

The Paint Bucket tool.

If you press the (Option)[Alt] key with the Paint Bucket tool selected, it toggles to the Eyedropper tool and vice versa. This makes it simple to quickly sample a color and apply it to other objects.

Summary

What a colorful hour! We learned all about the different kinds of colors Illustrator uses, and we learned how to create and edit swatches of colors. We also learned about two new palettes: the Swatches palette and the Color palette. Next hour, we learn what we can do with all of these wonderful colors.

Term Review

Color model—A specific defined color space such as CMYK, RGB, or HSB.

Custom color—A color defined in Illustrator that separates to its own plate. See Spot color.

Spot color—A specified color that is independent of any other colors in a job, and separates to its own plate.

Swatch—Illustrator's metaphor for a defined color, pattern, or gradient.

Hour 10

Fills

As we mentioned before, a vector object in Illustrator has two attributes: A fill and a stroke. This chapter focuses on the fill attribute. Remember how, when you were little, you used to use crayons on coloring books, and you were so careful not to "go out of the lines?" Well, that's what a fill in Illustrator is—coloring an object, up until the boundary of the path. The good thing about Illustrator is that it never draws out of the lines—it's perfect every time—and you don't have to worry about sharpening the crayon. In this hour we discuss:

- ☐ Applying a fill to an object
- ☐ Gradient fills
- ☐ Pattern fills
- ☐ The Expand command

Solid Color Fills

A solid color fill is rather simple. Using the same crayon example as earlier, a solid color fill is akin to using one particular crayon for the interior of the object. In the last hour we learned how to define new colors in Illustrator, as well as how to apply them to objects.

There are two other kinds of fills in Illustrator: gradients and patterns. Here we discuss how to define and apply these kinds of fills.

Gradients

Gradients are a powerful feature in Illustrator, enabling you to specify a fill of different colors blending with each other. Illustrator can create a gradient between just two colors or up to 32 colors. Gradients can be used to achieve cool shading effects, to add dimension to objects, and are also a great design element (see Figure 10.1).

Figure 10.1.
Gradients used for shading and adding dimension.

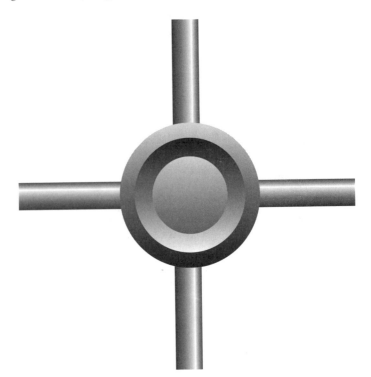

The Gradient Palette

You can apply a gradient by simply selecting a gradient swatch from the Swatches palette. To create or edit a gradient, however, you need to open the Gradient palette (F9). There you will find a gradient swatch, an option to make the gradient Linear or Radial, fields for Angle and Location, and a gradient slider (see Figure 10.2).

10

Figure 10.2.

The Gradient palette.

Defining a Gradient

You create a gradient much the same way you create a color. First, we define the gradient, and then we click the New Swatch icon in the Swatches palette. After you create the new swatch, it's important to double-click it and give it a name. Illustrator will just call it "Unnamed gradient," and after you have 15 unnamed gradients in your Swatches palette, you just *might* forget which one is which.

Notice that underneath the gradient slider are icons that look like little houses. These are *color stops* indicating the point at which a color is used in the gradient. To create a new color stop, click anywhere underneath the gradient slider. A new house appears that you can drag to the left or right. You can also drag any color from the Swatches or Color palettes onto the gradient slider to create a color stop in that color. To change an existing color stop, either drag a new color directly on top of it, or click the icon to select it, and change the color in the Color palette.

Also notice that there are little diamond-shaped icons on top of the gradient slider. These indicate the location of the midpoint of the gradation. In other words, wherever the diamond is, that's where there is 50% of each color (see Figure 10.3).

Figure 10.3.

Notice the color stops and location point indicators.

Let's define a gradient.

1. Open the Gradient palette (F9), the Color palette (F6), and the Swatches palette (F5).

2. In the Gradient palette, click the gradient swatch (it's the large square in the upper left of the palette). Notice that the gradient slider below becomes active, and the color stops and midpoint indicators become visible.

3. Click a color stop. There is now a color stop visible underneath the color swatch in the Color palette.

4. Using the sliders in the Color palette, or using the spectrum at the bottom of the Color palette, select a color for the selected color stop. Alternatively, you can drag a color from the Swatches palette directly onto the color stop in the Gradient palette.

5. Let's create a new color stop. Click anywhere directly underneath the gradient slider in the Gradient palette. Notice that another color stop appears. Apply a color to it the same way as in Step 4. Alternatively, you can drag a color from the Swatches palette directly onto the gradient slider. When you let go of the mouse, a color stop of the color you dragged appears.

6. Now let's delete a color stop. You need at least three color stops in order to delete one (a minimum of two color stops is required). Click and drag downwards on the color stop you want to delete. When the color stop disappears, release the mouse.

7. Now make your final adjustments by moving the color stops and the midpoint indicators.

8. Now that your gradient is complete, click the mouse on the gradient swatch and drag it into the Swatches palette, where it appears highlighted with a white outline.

9. Double-click the new swatch and give it an appropriate name. Click OK.

Editing a Gradient

To edit an existing gradient, modify the gradient in the Gradient palette, and then drag the gradient swatch on top of the swatch you want to update while holding down the (Option)[Alt] key.

The angle of the gradient can be changed in the Angle field in the Gradient palette. The angle does not affect the object in any way; it only affects the gradient that fills the object. In Figure 10.1, for example, 3D effects were achieved just by flipping the gradient 180 degrees.

Using the Gradient Tool

The Gradient tool is used to control the direction and placement of a gradient in an object or over several objects (see Figure 10.4). After an object is filled with a gradient, select the Gradient tool (G), and with the object still selected, click and drag across the object in the direction you wish the gradient to go. Where you begin dragging is where the gradient starts, and where you let go is where the gradient ends. If you stopped dragging before the end of the object, Illustrator continues to fill the object with the color at the end of the gradient. This tool is perfect for specifying where the center of a radial blend should be when making 3D spheres (see Figure 10.5).

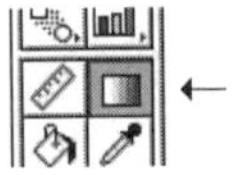

Figure 10.4.

The Gradient tool.

10

Figure 10.5.
*Using the Gradient tool,
you can make realistic
looking 3D spheres.*

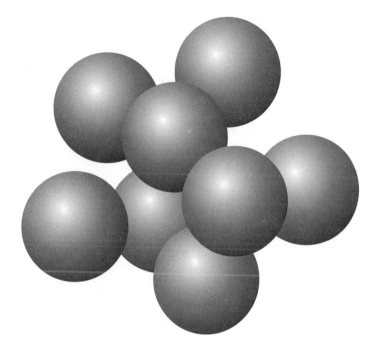

10

Patterns

Patterns can be real time savers. A pattern is a defined piece of art created in Illustrator that, as a fill attribute, is repeated over and over again, much like wallpaper (see Figure 10.6).

Defining a Pattern

Defining a pattern is a little different from defining gradients or colors. Instead of clicking the New Swatch icon, we drag our artwork directly into the Swatches palette to define the pattern. Again, after you create the swatch, give it a unique name so that you can find and edit it quickly.

When creating a pattern design, remember that your art will be repeated over and over again, so be careful how you set it up. If you need extra space around your art, create a box with a fill and stroke of none, and send it to the back of your artwork. Then, select your art along with the background box and define the pattern. Illustrator treats that empty box as the boundary for the pattern (see Figure 10.7).

Figure 10.6.

*Several pattern tiles and
what they look like when
used to fill an object.*

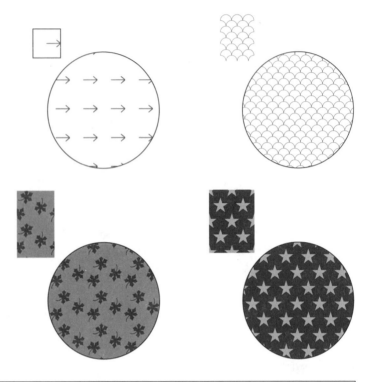

TIME SAVER

A pattern tile cannot contain another pattern or a gradient. If you want to
have a gradient effect or use a pattern within your pattern, use the Expand
command to convert the gradient or pattern into individual filled objects.
The Expand command is covered later in this hour.

To edit a pattern, drag the new artwork on top of the swatch you want to change while
pressing the (Option)[Alt] key. Also, if you lose the artwork for your pattern, don't worry.
If you drag a pattern swatch out of the Swatches palette and onto the page, it automatically
becomes the art for the pattern.

To move the pattern around within the object, select the object with the Selection tool, and
then click and drag the object while holding down the tilde (~) key. When you let go, only
the pattern is repositioned; the object does not move.

10

Figure 10.7.

The patterns with their bounding boxes (top) and the way they appear in a filled object (bottom).

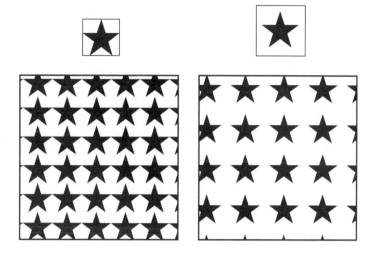

Using the Expand Command

Gradients, as we now know them, first appeared in Illustrator 5 for the Mac. In versions prior to that, you were able to achieve a gradated look by blending objects into each other. Basically, the Blend tool created many objects, or *steps*, each with a color slightly different than the next. This gave the appearance of a gradation. Of course, gradients are more intuitive and are easier to edit, but if you need to bring your artwork, which was created in version 7 with gradations, into version 3.2, you will lose the gradient information, as it is not supported in version 3.2.

In these circumstances, as well as others, you need to convert an object filled with a gradient into actual art or blended steps. To make this conversion, select the filled object and choose Expand Fill from the Object menu (see Figure 10.8). When expanding the gradient, you can specify how many steps Illustrator breaks it into.

Figure 10.8.

Choosing Expand Fill.

You can also expand an object filled with a pattern. By doing so, the fill that until now has been uneditable turns into actual art and ceases being a patterned fill. The shape also becomes a mask that blocks out parts of the pattern tiles that should not be visible (see Figure 10.9).

Figure 10.9.

From the top, a pattern and gradient as viewed in Preview mode, the same pattern and gradient viewed in Artwork mode, and finally, the same pattern and gradient viewed in Artwork mode after being expanded.

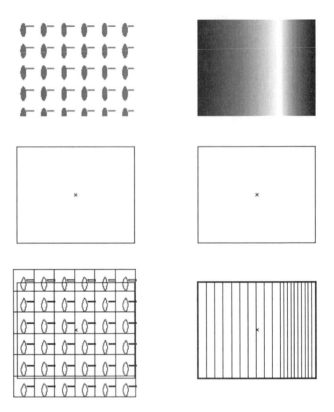

Summary

Are you all filled up? This hour we learned how to fill our shapes with not only flat solid colors but with interesting multicolor gradients and patterns as well. We also learned how to use the Expand feature to convert our gradients and patterns into editable art objects. Next hour we discuss the Stroke attribute.

Term Review

Gradient—Term used to describe a fill that contains two or more colors that blend into each other.

Color stop—The point in a gradient where a new color is introduced.

Steps—Individual parts of a blend. Each step is a slightly different color giving the illusion of a smooth transition.

10

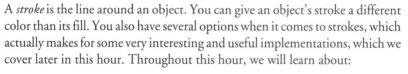

Hour 11

Strokes

A *stroke* is the line around an object. You can give an object's stroke a different color than its fill. You also have several options when it comes to strokes, which actually makes for some very interesting and useful implementations, which we cover later in this hour. Throughout this hour, we will learn about:

☐ The Stroke palette

☐ Stroke weights, miters, and caps

☐ Dashed lines

☐ Layered strokes

The Stroke Palette

The Stroke palette (F10) can be set to either show only the stroke weight or all of the stroke attributes including Miter Limit, Line Caps and Joins, and Dashed Lines. You can choose either setting by selecting *Show Options* from the palette menu (see Figure 11.1).

Figure 11.1.

*Viewing the entire Stroke
palette.*

Weight and Miter Limit

The most used option in the Stroke palette is the stroke weight. This is what determines how thick or thin the stroke is. Illustrator's default is 1 point. For hairline rules, most people use .25 point. You can enter any amount from 0 to 1000 points, and you can even enter numbers in different measurements (such as 2.5 in.) and Illustrator converts it to points for you.

CAUTION

In Illustrator, if you enter a weight of zero points, it prints the stroke as a PostScript Hairline, which is defined as the smallest line width possible on your printing device. This means if you are printing to a 300 dpi laser printer, your "0" point stroke prints at 1/300 of an inch. Print that same "0" point stroke on a high-end 3386 dpi imagesetter and you get a stroke of 1/3386 of an inch, which is barely discernible, even using a 10 × loupe. My advice is to avoid using "0" point, and when you want a hairline, use .25 point. You'll be happy you did.

The Miter Limit determines how far the stroke sticks out on a sharp point. A thick line, for example, needs more room to complete a sharp point than a thin one does (see Figure 11.2).

Figure 11.2.

*From the left, a 2 point
stroke with a miter limit
of 2, a 20 point stroke
with a miter limit of 2,
and a 20 point stroke
with a miter limit of 4.*

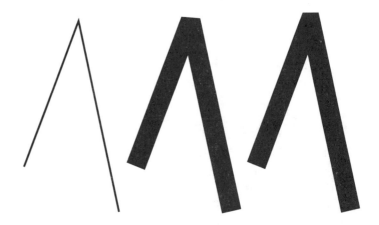

11

Line Caps and Joins

Line caps determine the ends of a stroked path. This setting is only used for open-ended paths. By choosing different caps, you can make the ends either flat, rounded, or have the stroke width enclose the end of the path as well (see Figure 11.3).

Figure 11.3.

The three types of line caps. Notice how the bottom two actually protrude one-half the stroke weight from the actual anchor point.

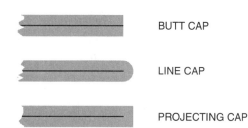

BUTT CAP

LINE CAP

PROJECTING CAP

Line joins control how the stroke appears at each anchor point on the path. You can choose Mitered, Round, or Beveled joins (see Figure 11.4).

Figure 11.4.

A star with (from left) mitered, round, and beveled joins.

Dashed Lines

The last option in the Stroke palette can be one of the most powerful. Here you can specify dashed or dotted lines. Depending on what settings you have set for weight, line caps, and joins, you can create a stitched line, a skip line, or almost anything. You control the dash and gap (the space between each dash) by entering numbers into the Dash and Gap fields at the bottom of the palette. If you're just using one sequence, you can enter just the first two fields. Or you can enter up to three different Dash and Gap settings to achieve complex dash patterns (see Figure 11.5).

Figure 11.5.

A variety of strokes with different Dash and Gap settings. The last stroke uses round caps to achieve the dotted line effect.

(1, 6, 6, 1)	▪ ━ ▪━ ▪━ ▪━ ▪━ ▪━ ▪━ ▪━ ▪━ ▪
(2, 10, 10, 10)	▪ ━ ▪ ━ ▪ ━ ▪ ━ ▪ ━ ▪
(2, 8,8)	▪ ━ ▪ ━ ▪ ━ ▪ ━ ▪ ━
(12, 2)	━ ━ ━ ━ ━ ━ ━ ━
(4, 2, 4, 20)	▪▪ ▪▪ ▪▪ ▪▪ ▪▪
(1, 6 – Round Cap)	• • • • • • • • • • • • • • • • • • •

Creating Special Effects with Layered Strokes

Using strokes with different settings, and layering them on top of each other, you can achieve some interesting results. How interesting, you ask? Well, how about railroad tracks? or maybe a nice highway? With some imagination and forethought, you can apply the power of strokes to more and more functions. The possibilities are endless!

Everybody's Doing the Locomotion

1. With the Freehand tool, draw a nice squiggly line with a fill of None and a stroke of black (see Figure 11.6).

Figure 11.6.

Start with a nice curved line.

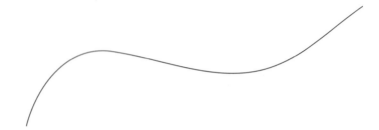

2. Give it a stroke weight of 20 points, and a miter limit of 4 (see Figure 11.7).

Figure 11.7.

I've been workin' on the railroad...

3. Press (Command-C)[Control-C] to copy the path, and then press (Command-F)[Control-F] to paste the path directly in front of the existing path. (You won't see a change onscreen, but it's there.)
4. Give this path a fill of None and a stroke of white.
5. Change the stroke weight to 14 points. You should now see a double line (see Figure 11.8). Because the white line is narrower, you see 3 points of the bottom line on either side (20 minus 14).

11

Figure 11.8.

In reality, what you're seeing is a white line blocking out the middle of a thicker black stroke.

6. Again, press (Command-C)[Control-C] and then (Command-F)[Control-F] to create another copy of the path.

7. Give the path a fill of None, and a stroke of black.

8. Change the weight to 26 points, and give the stroke a dash of 2 points and a gap of 10 points (see Figure 11.9).

Figure 11.9.

The completed train tracks.

Look at that! We created train tracks from just three paths. Even more amazing, switch to artwork mode (Command-Y)[Control-Y] and what do you see? Only one thin line.

Life in the Illustrator Fast Lane

Think that's cool? Well, my good friend Ted Alspach of Illustrator fame put together something even cooler: an *eight lane freeway*, made up entirely of strokes.

1. Draw a path with the Pen tool that looks like the one shown. You can make your path longer if you'd like; I've created a path that's fairly short so it looks good in the sample figures.

2. Change the paint style (Fill=none; Stroke=300 pt., C=100, M=10, Y=90, K=18). This path is the grass border of the highway.

3. Copy (Command-C)[Control-C] and Paste in Front (Command-F)[Control-F]. Change the paint style (Stroke=240 pt., K=80). This is the dark asphalt edge of the highway.

4. Paste in Front (Command-F)[Control-F]. Change the paint style (Stroke=165 pt., white). This is the white line along the outside edge of the highway.

5. Paste in Front (Command-F)[Control-F]. Change the paint style (Stroke=160 pt., K=40). This path is the main road.

6. Paste in Front (Command-F)[Control-F]. Change the paint style (Stroke=85 pt., white, dash=12, gap=20). Though it doesn't look like it right now, these are the dashed lines.

7. Paste in Front (Command-F)[Control-F]. Change the paint style (Stroke=80 pt., K=40). This is the passing lane.

8. Paste in Front (Command-F)[Control-F]. Change the paint style (Stroke=8 pt., M=10, Y=100). This is the double yellow line.

9. Paste in Front (Command-F)[Control-F]. Change the paint style (Stroke=3 pt., K=40). This path is used to separate the double yellow lines.

Shown here are two variations on the highway theme. The first is a two lane highway, while the second is an intricate eight lane freeway.

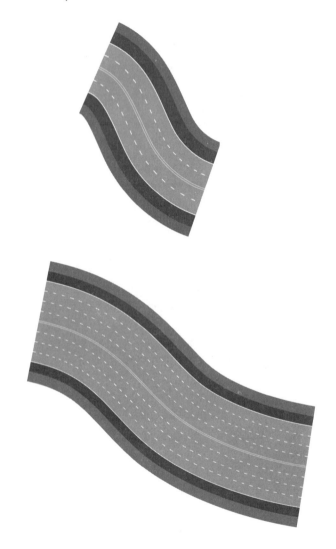

Offset Path and Outline Path

For outlining and special effects, Offset Path is a great function. Offset Path creates an object that perfectly outlines, or traces, a selected path at an offset that you specify. To use it, select one or more objects and choose Object➤Path➤Offset Path (see Figure 11.10) and the Offset Path dialog box appears (see Figure 11.11). Enter an amount to offset (you can use positive or negative numbers), and click OK. Note that Offset Path always makes a copy of your selection, and does not affect the original (see Figure 11.12).

Figure 11.10.
Choosing Offset Path from the Object menu.

Figure 11.11.
You can select one of three join options: round, bevel, and miter.

Figure 11.12.
The results of using Offset Path.

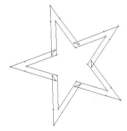

TIME SAVER

You may notice that the Offset Path command may produce what looks like extra lines in each object (refer to Figure 11.12). To "clean up" these lines choose Object➡Pathfinder➡Unite. It's best to run this function right after you use Offset Path because your selection is still active. (More on the Unite and Pathfinder commands in Hour 13, "The Pathfinder Commands.")

Outline Path is another great feature that converts strokes into filled objects (see Figure 11.13). Found in the same location as the Offset Path command, the Outline Path works by taking the stroke width and creating a filled shape the size of the width (see Figure 11.14). This can be a real timesaver in a production environment, as well as enable workarounds such as filling an outlined stroke with a gradient (a gradient cannot be applied to a stroke).

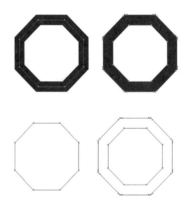

Figure 11.13.
On the left, a stroked path. On the right, the path converted to an outline.

Figure 11.14.
With the same images viewed in Artwork mode, you can see how the stroke has been outlined.

Unfortunately, Outline Path does not use dash information when converting a path to an outline. When used, the path (actually the object) becomes solid.

11

Summary

Before things even got started, we learned that strokes are a good thing (at least in Illustrator they are). We learned all about stroke weight, and how different joins and caps can make a stroke appear very different. After we covered dashed patterns, we even made an entire illustration out of nothing but strokes!

Term Review

Stroke weight—The thickness of a line (path).

Miter—The extrusion of the stroke weight at a sharp change in direction.

Cap—The stroke attribute used at the endpoints of a stroke.

Dash—The part of a stroke that is visible.

Gap—The part of a stroke that is transparent.

Stitched Line—A steady dashed line, giving the appearance of a sewn stitch.

Skip Line—A dashed line in which the dash and gap are not consistent.

Hour **12**

Transformations

One of the biggest advantages computers give us in terms of creating art is the ability to edit or transform art. I remember when I used to draw squares for a layout, and send out for several copies of them to save time when doing layout. Now I can create numerous duplicates of art in nanoseconds. By scaling, rotating, and reflecting existing art, we not only cut production times in half, but we create better, more accurate art as well (see Figure 12.1). In this hour we discuss:

- ☐ Moving
- ☐ Scaling
- ☐ Rotating
- ☐ Reflecting
- ☐ Shearing

Figure 12.1.
By drawing only half of the image, and then reflecting a copy of it, you can create a symmetrical image in half the time.

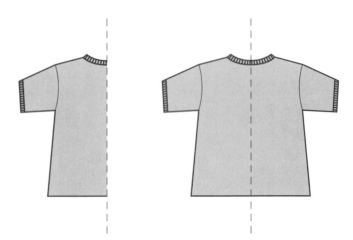

The Transformation Tools

Illustrator has five transformation functions: Move, Rotate, Scale, Reflect, and Shear. Illustrator 7 also has a new feature called Transform Each that enables you to apply several different transformations to several different objects—all in one step. There's also the Transform palette, which makes for quick and precise transformations.

Before we begin, I want to point out one particular keyboard shortcut that is a real time-saver—especially when it comes to transformations. Pressing the (Command)[Control] key at any time activates the most recent selection tool you've used. If, for example, you last used the black arrow, pressing the (Command)[Control] key while using any of Illustrator's other tools temporarily activates the black arrow.

When it comes to transformations, you are always selecting objects and making minor changes to the art, and it's a pain to have to switch back and forth between the transformation tools and the selection tools. With the (Command)[Control] key, the selection tool is always just a keystroke away. By the way, pressing (Command-Tab)[Control-Tab] toggles between the black and white arrow.

Moving Objects

Although not necessarily a transformation in that the actual *object* is changed, moving an image is considered a transformation because the *coordinates* of the object are being changed.

To demonstrate, press F8 to open the Info palette (see Figure 12.2). Now, select the Rectangle tool (press R) and move your mouse around the screen. There are four fields in the Info

12

palette: X, Y, W, and H. Notice the X and Y numbers are changing as you move the mouse. These are the coordinates of your cursor and they represent the starting point of your rectangle (either the center point or the upper-left point, depending on which rectangle tool you are using). After you begin drawing the rectangle, the other W and H (width and height) coordinates become active, giving you real-time feedback as to the size of your object.

Figure 12.2.

Illustrator's Info palette:
In this example the
measurements are shown
in inches, as per my
setting in Preferences (see
Hour 2, "Customizing
Illustrator").

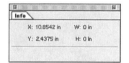

We already learned one way to move an object; by clicking and dragging on a selection. Illustrator also lets you move things more precisely. If you click and drag a selection, and *then* hold down the Shift key, you are only able to drag your selection in increments of 45 degrees.

Want to get even more precise? After you make your selection, you can use your keyboard's arrows (up, down, left and right) to "nudge" your selection, one increment at a time. You can control how much each nudge is in the Keyboard Shortcuts section in Preferences (see Figure 12.3).

Figure 12.3.

The value in the Cursor
Key field determines how
much a "nudge" is.

But you say you need even *more* precision? After all, we *are* dealing with a computer, right? To move a selection numerically, make your selection and then double-click the Selection tool in the Toolbox (the black arrow). You are presented with a dialog box where you can specify an exact amount to three decimal places (see Figure 12.4). The dialog box also lets you create a copy, and even sports a Preview button that enables you to view the results of the move before clicking OK.

Figure 12.4.

*Double-clicking the black
arrow brings up the
Move dialog box.*

There's yet another way to move something: Illustrator's new Transform palette, which we get to soon.

Rotate, Scale, Reflect, and Shear

The remaining four transformation tools, Rotate, Scale, Reflect, and Shear, are all very similar. As you should know by now, before making any transformations, you must first make a selection. Otherwise, Illustrator has no idea what it is you want to transform. A rectangle works best for demonstration purposes.

Rotate

When you select the Rotate tool (R), notice that a different symbol has appeared at the center of your selection (see Figure 12.5). This is your origin point. With the Rotate tool, your origin point is the rotation point, which means your selection revolves around that point. To rotate the object, simply click and drag (see Figure 12.6). Clicking the outer portion of a selection makes it easier to control the transformation. Holding the Shift key while dragging constrains your rotation to increments of 45 degrees.

Figure 12.5.

*Besides the usual selection
points, when performing
a transformation,
Illustrator indicates the
origin point.*

Figure 12.6.

*Notice the object rotates
around the origin point.*

You can move the origin point to better control your transformations by clicking and dragging it. Go ahead, try it! Drag the origin point to the lower-left corner of the rectangle (see Figure 12.7). Notice that the origin point takes advantage of Snap to Point, which makes aligning images a lot easier to do. Now click and drag from the opposite side of the rectangle, and notice how the object now rotates from the lower-left corner (see Figure 12.8).

12

Figure 12.7.

Repositioning the origin point.

Figure 12.8.

The object, being rotated around the newly placed origin point.

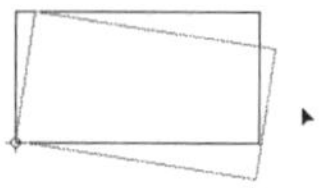

Besides being able to freely rotate a selection, you can also precisely rotate an object numerically. To do so, double-click the Rotate tool. This brings up the Rotate dialog box (see Figure 12.9). After specifying a rotation angle, you can choose OK to rotate your selection, or you can choose Copy, which rotates a duplicate of your selection, and leave the original selection untouched (see Figure 12.10).

Figure 12.9.

The Rotate dialog box.

Figure 12.10.

Clicking Copy transforms a duplicate while leaving the original untouched.

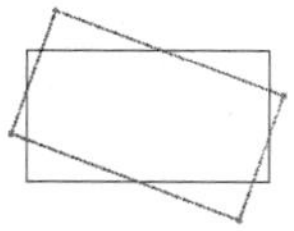

Double-clicking the Rotate tool always rotates the selection numerically from the center, but what if you want to rotate a selection numerically from a different origin point? After you have the Rotate tool selected, hold down the (Option)[Alt] key and click where you want the origin point to be. The Rotate dialog box appears, and the origin point is where you clicked.

TIME SAVER

When using the Rotate dialog box, if the object you are rotating is filled with a pattern, you have the option to rotate the object without rotating the pattern, to rotate the pattern and the object simultaneously, or to rotate just the pattern (see Figure 12.11). Without using the dialog box, you can rotate just the pattern fill if you press and hold the tilde key (~) while dragging to rotate. The tilde key shortcut works with any of the transformation tools, including Move.

12

Figure 12.11.

From left to right, the original object, the object rotated without the fill, the object and the fill rotated together, and the fill rotated without the object.

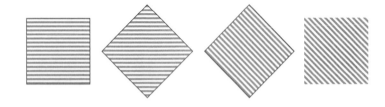

Scale

Probably the most frequently used transformation tool, the Scale tool (S) is used to resize selected objects, making them larger or smaller. Just like the Rotate tool, the Scale tool also uses an origin point to determine which point to scale from.

Figure 12.12.

Illustrator's Scale tool.

To use the Scale tool, drag inward toward the origin point to reduce the object in size. Drag outward from the origin point to enlarge the object. You can move the origin point by pressing and dragging it or just clicking to create a new origin point. If you hold down the Shift key as you drag, the object scales proportionally.

To scale items from the center, numerically, double-click the Scale tool to bring up the Scale dialog box (see Figure 12.13). Although Scale line weight appears in General Preferences (see Hour 2), it appears here again, in case you want to make an exception (see Figure 12.14).

Figure 12.13.

The Scale dialog box.

As with the Rotate tool, if you want to scale a selection numerically, but from a specified origin point, select the Scale tool and (Option-click)[Alt-click] where you want the origin point to be.

Reflect

The Reflect tool (O) is also known as the mirror tool (see Figure 12.15). Working in the same way as the Rotate and Scale tools, the Reflect tool flips a selection horizontally or vertically. This tool is most useful for creating symmetrical artwork. After creating half of your art, simply flip a copy of it to complete the image (see Figure 12.16).

12

Figure 12.14.

The box on the left has been reduced with Scale line weight off. The box on the right has Scale line weight turned on. It appears to be an optical illusion, but the stroke has remained the same in the first example and been scaled proportionally in the second.

Figure 12.15.

Illustrator's Reflect tool.

Figure 12.16.

By using the Reflect tool, you can create a perfect image in half the time.

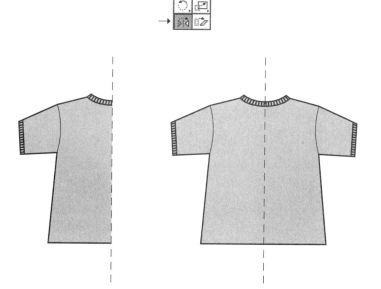

As with the other transformation tools, holding the Shift key constrains movement to 45 degree increments, and double-clicking the Reflect tool or (Option-clicking)[Alt-clicking] in the document brings up the Reflect dialog box (see Figure 12.17).

Figure 12.17.

The Reflect dialog box.

Shear

The last of the transformation tools, the Shear tool (W), as shown in Figure 12.18, is used to skew objects (see Figure 12.19). Again, this transformation tool is like the others when it comes to specifying an origin point, and using the Shift key. Of course, double-clicking the Shear tool brings up the Shear dialog box (see Figure 12.20), and (Option-clicking)[Alt-clicking] in your document defines an origin point and enables you to specify a shear numerically.

Figure 12.18.

Illustrator's Shear tool.

 ←

Figure 12.19.

A square that has been sheared. Notice that by shearing a copy of the star, I can create a cast shadow.

Figure 12.20.

The Shear dialog box.

Transform Each

The Transform Each function offers two excellent features: the ability to perform Scale, Move, and Rotate transformations simultaneously; and the ability to transform each object in a selection independently of each other. Let's take a closer look.

12

First, multiple transformations are a snap with Transform Each. Choose Object➡Transform➡Transform Each (see Figure 12.21) to bring up the Transform Each dialog box (see Figure 12.22). Here you can specify measurements for Scaling, Moving, and Rotating your selection. A Preview button enables you to view your transformation in real-time. We'll see in a minute how this feature is more powerful than you think.

Figure 12.21.

Choosing Transform Each.

Figure 12.22.

The Transform Each dialog box.

The second feature we mentioned was the ability to transform multiple objects individually. To demonstrate, I've created a grid of squares (see Figure 12.23). If I select all of the squares, and use the Rotate tool to rotate my selection 45 degrees, my entire selection rotates as one piece (see Figure 12.24). If I use the Transform Each command with the same selection and specify a 45-degree rotation, however, each square rotates individually (see Figure 12.25).

Figure 12.23.

Many squares.

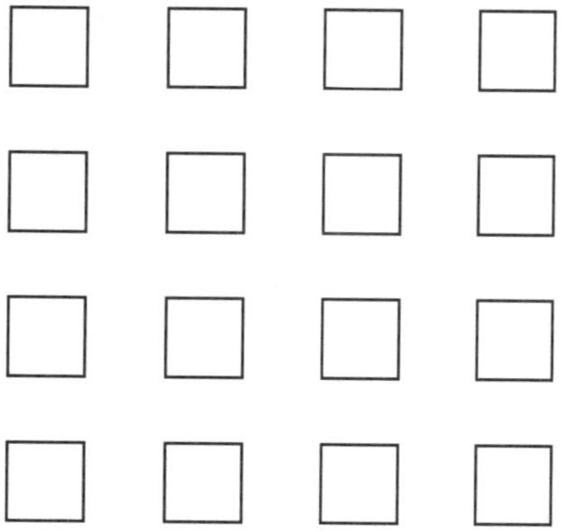

12

Figure 12.24.
A normal rotate rotates all objects around the center point of the entire selection.

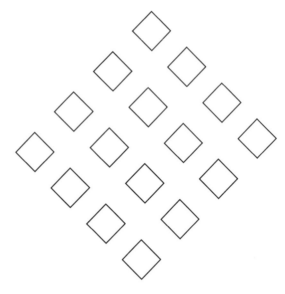

Figure 12.25.
Transform Each rotates each square around its own center.

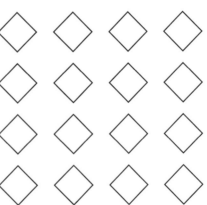

The Random button in the Transform Each dialog box transforms each object a little differently, making for an irregular, almost hand-drawn look (see Figure 12.26).

12

Figure 12.26.

Using Transform Each's
Random feature.

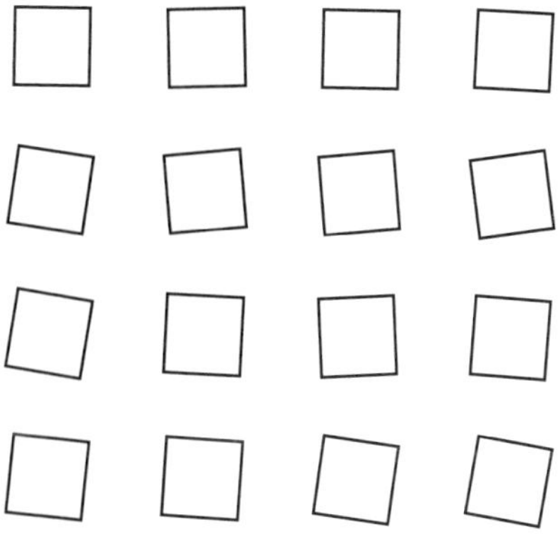

Makin' Copies!

As you've seen in all of the transformation dialog boxes, there is a button to make the transformation on a copy of the object. Holding the (Option)[Alt] button as you drag with any transformation tool does the same thing. If you want to rotate a copy of a selection, just hold down the (Option)[Alt] key as you drag to rotate. Even when dragging items with the black or white arrows, holding the (Option)[Alt] key creates a duplicate. Be sure to release the mouse button before you let go of the (Option)[Alt] key.

Do It Again!

Without a doubt, the most powerful transform function in Illustrator is Transform Again. The keystroke combination for it is (Command-D)[Control-D]. Learn it. Transform Again applies the last transform that you've done, which is why Sandee Cohen, of vector fame, likes to call the function "Do It Again," which also makes it easier to remember (Command-D)[Control-D]. Let's do a few simple exercises:

1. Draw a rectangle.

2. Using the black arrow, move the square a bit.

3. Press (Command-D)[Control-D]. Notice how Illustrator applied the same move command to the square again.

4. Now rotate the square 20 degrees (see Figure 12.27).

12

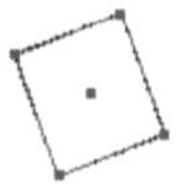

Figure 12.27.

Rotating the square.

5. Press (Command-D)[Control-D] again. And again. The square rotates another 20 degrees each time (see Figure 12.28).

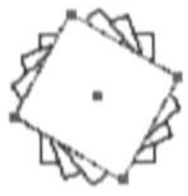

Figure 12.28.

Getting dizzy?

6. Select the black arrow again.
7. Now create a duplicate of the square by clicking and dragging it while holding the (Option)[Alt] key (see Figure 12.29).

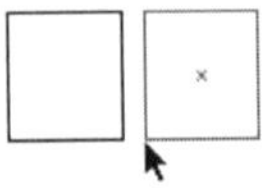

Figure 12.29.

Duplicating the square.

8. Press (Command-D)[Control-D] several times. You just performed a step-and-repeat, creating several squares, each equally distant from the other (see Figure 12.30).

Figure 12.30.

Many squares.

Now let's go back to the Transform Each function. Remember, using Transform Each, we can apply several transformations in one step. Using the Transform Again function in conjunction with Transform Each gives us a powerful means to apply multiple transformations again and again—quickly.

The Transform Palette

You knew it was coming, didn't you? That's right, another Illustrator palette. The Transform palette lets you quickly specify transformations (see Figure 12.31).

First, notice the funny-looking icon on the far left (see Figure 12.32). This is a proxy that determines where the origin point is. Although you can't precisely position the origin point as you could with a transform tool, clicking the little squares lets you quickly specify center, upper-left corner, and so on.

Figure 12.31.
The Transform palette.

Figure 12.32.
The Transform Proxy for determining the origin point.

You can move objects around in your document by entering the X and Y coordinates. To change the width and height of your selected objects, enter new values in the W and H fields. But what if you only know one dimension and want to transform your object proportionally? Let's say, for example, you want to make your object 3 inches wide. Put 3 inches in the W field and then hold down the (Command)[Control] key and press Enter. Illustrator automatically figures out the correct height, scaling your object proportionally.

There are also fields for rotation and shearing. If you hold down the (Option)[Alt] key when pressing enter, Illustrator creates a duplicate and leaves the original item untouched.

The Align Palette

Because we're talking all about moving things around, I thought now might be a good time to introduce you to the Align palette (yet *another* Illustrator palette to deal with). The Align palette, as shown in Figure 12.33, was at one time a list of commands under the Filter menu. As a palette, it is much easier to use and understand. To use it, simply select your objects and click any of the Align or Distribute buttons. Distribute works by taking the two outermost objects, and then evenly spacing the objects that appear between them. To center two objects vertically and horizontally, for example, you would click the *Horizontal Align Center* button, and then the *Vertical Align Center* button (see Figure 12.34).

Figure 12.33.
The Align palette.

Figure 12.34.
From left to right: the original objects, after horizontally aligning them, and then after vertically aligning them.

12

Summary

Today was topsy-turvy day. We flipped, flopped, turned, moved, rotated, scaled, slanted, and jolted. We also learned about some new palettes, plus some pretty cool features, such as (Command-D)[Control-D] and Transform Each.

Term Review

Scale—The act of resizing an object.

Rotate—The act of making an object turn on a 2-dimensional axis.

Reflect—The act of flipping an object to create a mirror image.

Shear—The act of skewing an object, giving the appearance of a slant.

Align—Command used to align objects in respect to each other.

Distribute—Command used to evenly distribute objects throughout a specified distance.

12

Hour 13

The Pathfinder Commands

If you were to ask me what the best feature in Illustrator is, I would tell you the Pathfinder functions. One of the greatest time-saving features in Illustrator, the Pathfinder commands are a set of powerful path-editing functions found under the Object menu (see Figure 13.1). In this hour we cover these functions, including:

- ☐ Unite
- ☐ Divide
- ☐ Crop
- ☐ Trap

Once a set of filters (since version 5.5), the Pathfinder commands enable you to quickly perform complex path functions on multiple objects. Later, we describe each function, as well as present an example to demonstrate what each command does.

Unite, Intersect, Exclude, Minus Front, Minus Back

The first group of Pathfinder commands is used to make complex shapes out of simple ones (see Figure 13.2). You can quickly create unique art by using Illustrator's basic drawing tools, and then modify them using these Pathfinder commands.

Figure 13.1.

*Choosing the Pathfinder
commands.*

Figure 13.2.

*The first set of Pathfinder
commands.*

Unite

The most commonly used Pathfinder command, Unite simply takes all selected objects and combines them into one object. Unite doesn't just group the objects together; it "glues" them all together, leaving just one large shape, removing all paths that overlap (see Figure 13.3). When running the Unite command, the final object is automatically brought to the front. Whatever color the front-most object in your selection is becomes the color of the final, united object.

Figure 13.3.

*The Unite command
combines objects.*

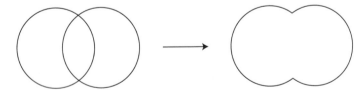

Intersect

The Intersect function is used on two objects that overlap each other. After you choose Intersect, the area in which the objects overlap remains as one combined path, and the rest of each object is deleted (see Figure 13.4). This command won't work if you have more than two objects selected.

13

Figure 13.4.
The overlapping portion remains.

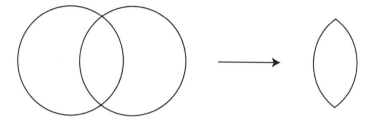

Exclude

The exact opposite of the Intersect command, Exclude takes two objects that overlap each other and deletes the areas where they overlap (see Figure 13.5). The remaining objects are grouped together. This command won't work if you have more than two objects selected.

Figure 13.5.
Removing the overlapping portion.

Minus Front

Minus Front takes two objects and subtracts the front-most object from the object behind it (see Figure 13.6). This command is great for cutting little shapes or bits out of larger objects. If the front image fits within the back image, Minus Front creates a compound path for you. It works a lot like a cookie cutter, only what you end up seeing is what's left of the dough, not the cookie. This command won't work if you have more than two objects selected.

Figure 13.6.
Removing the front object, and whatever is behind it.

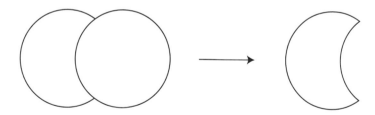

13

Minus Back

The reverse of Minus Front, Minus Back subtracts part of an image based on the image behind it (see Figure 13.7). Going back to the cookie cutter example, this filter would produce the cookie. This command won't work if you have more than two objects selected.

Figure 13.7.

Removing the rear object and taking whatever is in front of it with it.

Divide, Outline, Trim, Merge, and Crop

The next group of Pathfinder commands deals with splitting objects into parts or deleting unwanted parts of objects (see Figure 13.8).

Figure 13.8.

The second batch of Pathfinder commands.

Divide

Divide takes any overlapping shapes and cuts them up into separate shapes wherever they overlap (see Figure 13.9). An invaluable tool, Divide enables you to quickly split up objects without once having to use the Scissors tool. Also, using the precision of drawn shapes, you can perform careful slices and divisions without using the clumsy Knife tool.

Figure 13.9.

Divide turns each intersecting part into a separate image.

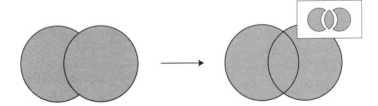

Divide looks at each object and divides each overlap individually, so it makes no difference if you're dividing compound paths, groups, or whatever—they all become individual shapes. After Divide runs, all objects are grouped together. You have to ungroup them if you want to work with each piece separately.

Outline

Choosing the Outline command converts all shapes to outlines (see Figure 13.10), and also divides the lines where they intersect (similar to a Divide command for strokes).

13

Figure 13.10.
The Outline command.

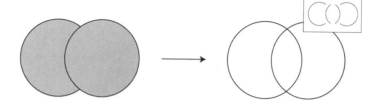

Trim

The Trim command removes the parts of the back object that are behind the front objects. It also removes the stroke (see Figure 13.11).

Figure 13.11.
Running the Trim command.

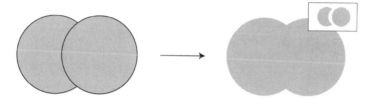

Merge

The Merge command operates differently, depending on the fills of the selected objects. If they're all the same, it's similar to Unite, making them one object. If they're all different, it works like the Trim command, mentioned above. If some of the objects are filled the same, the like objects are united, and the rest are trimmed (see Figure 13.12).

Figure 13.12.
Running the Merge command.

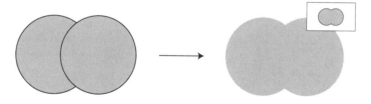

13

Crop

The Crop command removes any parts of selected objects that are not directly underneath the front-most object (see Figure 13.13). The final result of the Crop command is exactly what a mask would do. The only difference is, the Crop command actually deletes the art that is not visible, unlike a mask, which just covers it up. Be careful before you run this command, because you cannot retrieve the artwork that is cropped out.

Figure 13.13.
The Crop command.

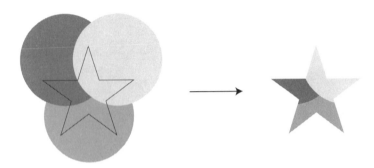

Hard and Soft

One of the most common uses for these two commands is for simulating transparency effects. These filters mix overlapping colors.

Hard

The Hard command takes overlapping objects and mixes the values of the colors where the shapes overlap (see Figure 13.14).

Figure 13.14.
Mixing colors with the Hard command.

Soft

The Soft command is identical to the Hard command, except for the fact that you can control how the colors are mixed by specifying a percentage. Although Hard might produce an image that looks transparent, Soft might be used to create an object that appears translucent (see Figure 13.15).

Figure 13.15.
Creating a translucent effect with the Soft command.

13

Trap

The Trap command takes selected art and *traps* it as specified (see Figure 13.16). Many printers today require that you provide artwork that is trapped properly. It is best to speak with your printer and discuss your options. If you need to trap your own artwork, make sure your printer provides you with the settings he needs.

Figure 13.16.

The Pathfinder Trap dialog box.

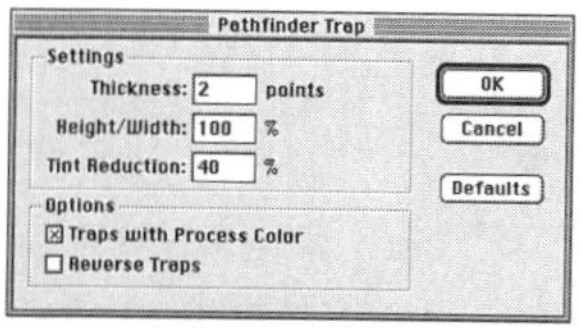

A computer is perfect. When you draw a square of one color and place it right up against another square of another color, you get two squares touching each other, with one color ending where the next one begins.

Out in the real world, however, this is not always so easy. A printing press is (usually) a large machine, and it's nearly impossible for every color to print in the exact same place every time. What usually happens, in our case with the squares, is that there is a slight shift between the colors that enables a sliver of white, or whatever color the paper is, to sneak through between the two squares.

To get around this problem, printers rely on a process called *trapping*. By slightly extending the colors (called *choking* and *spreading*) and having them *overprint* each other, the squares do not just touch each other, but actually overlap a bit. Now, if the press shifts a bit, there is enough of an overlap of color that a white sliver won't show through. By setting a color to overprint, you are instructing the colors to print over each other, achieving the trap.

Because the Trap command makes changes to your artwork, it's a good idea to save a copy of your file before you use it. Also, save it for the last step to make for easier editing.

Overprints

Because we're mentioning traps, I thought I'd also show you how you can specify *overprints* through Illustrator's Attributes palette (see Figure 13.17). After you select an object, you can choose to overprint the fill or the stroke by checking the appropriate box.

Figure 13.17.

The Attributes palette.

One More Shortcut

Before we wrap things up, I'd just like to point out that (Command-4)[Control-4] performs the last-used Pathfinder command. Many times when editing multiple objects, you need to apply Pathfinder commands over and over again, and it's a bit of a pain going all the way into the Pathfinder submenu so often. (Extensis VectorTools 2.0 has a floating palette with all of Illustrator's Pathfinder commands).

Summary

Pathfinder rules! Today we learned how the Pathfinder commands slice, dice, mince, chop, and mix together all of our favorite vector recipes. We even dived right into a conversation about trapping and overprinting. And if all this wasn't enough for you, the next hour talks about using text in Illustrator.

Term Review

Trapping—The process of spreading or extending colors to compensate for printing press error.

Overprinting—Technical term for forcing one color to print on top of another.

Hour 14

Adding Text

Illustrator would be incomplete without text capabilities. No matter if it's designing a logo, creating a headline and body copy for an ad, or creating a caption for a technical illustration, Illustrator can handle it. Text alone can also be a powerful way of graphic expression. Illustrator works with type in a variety of ways, and as we go through this hour, you learn where and when to use each one. Topics this hour covers include:

- ☐ Point text
- ☐ Area text
- ☐ Text on a path

JUST A MINUTE

Before we begin using the Type tool, let me remind you that there is an option in your Preferences dialog box on how to select type: Type Area Select. With Type Area Select activated you can select text by clicking with the Selection or Direct Selection tool anywhere within the type's bounding box. With Type Area Select turned off, you must click the baseline to select the type. If you have trouble selecting type because other objects get in the way, lock or hide those objects first, and then you can select and edit your type easily.

Using the Type Tool

Illustrator has three types of text: point text, area text, and text on a path. To create text in Illustrator, you use one of the many type tools, found in the Toolbox (see Figure 14.1).

Figure 14.1.

A multitude of type tools.

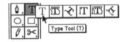

Point Text

The most popular kind of text in Illustrator is point text. Also called headline text, point text is defined by a single point, meaning that justification (such as left, right, or centered text) is based on that one point (see Figure 14.2). Creating point text is also very easy: with the Type tool selected (T), just click a blank area anywhere on the page and start typing.

Figure 14.2.

Although the points are aligned vertically, the type can be aligned to the right, center, or left of the point.

Editing Text

After you create the text, you can edit it by simply using the Text tool to click and drag on letters. This highlights the text (see Figure 14.3), and typing something new replaces the highlighted text. To simply add text to an existing block of type, click where you want the type to begin, and a blinking cursor appears, ready for you to add text.

Figure 14.3.
The "T" is selected.

Hello **T**here!

14

Area Text

Area text, also called body text, is defined by a shape—much like QuarkXPress where all type must be within a frame (see Figure 14.4).

Figure 14.4.

Type within a circle.

AS HARRY CHAPIN SANG, "ALL MY LIFE'S A CIRCLE, SUNRISE AND SUNDOWN. THE MOON ROLLS THROUGH THE NIGHTTIME, TILL THE DAYBREAK COMES AROUND. ALL MY LIFE'S A CIRCLE BUT I CAN'T TELL YOU WHY, SEASONS SPINNING ROUND AGAIN THE YEARS KEEP GOIN' BY"

You can create area text in several ways:

- ☐ With the Area Type tool selected (see Figure 14.5), click an existing path. Any type you enter fills the interior of the path.

- ☐ With the Type tool selected, click and drag diagonally to draw a box (see Figure 14.6).

- ☐ With the Type tool selected, click an existing path. As you drag your cursor over a path, notice it changes to the Area Type tool cursor (see Figure 14.7).

Figure 14.5.

Selecting the Area Type tool from the Toolbox.

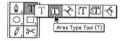

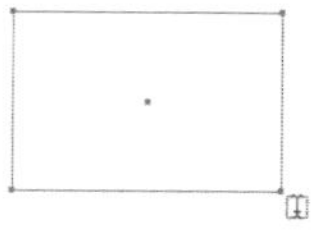

Figure 14.6.

Drawing a text box with the Type tool.

14

Figure 14.7.

*Dragging the Type tool
icon over a path turns it
into the Area Type tool
icon.*

Linking Text Blocks

If you have more type than can fit into the selected shape, a small plus sign in a box appears
at the lower right of the shape (see Figure 14.8). The symbol indicates that there is more text
that overflows from the shape.

Figure 14.8.

*The little plus sign
symbol indicates a text
overflow.*

Illustrator enables you to *link* shapes so that overflow type from the first shape flows into the
next shape. You can do this by selecting the object with the overflowing type, along with the
object you want to link it to. Then choose Type➧Link➧Blocks (see Figure 14.9).

Figure 14.9.

Linked text blocks.

Rows and Columns

All this talk about linking text blocks reminds me about a wonderful feature in Illustrator
called Rows and Columns. Although you can't create columns of text within one text block,
you can create several blocks of type and link them. This handy feature makes creating rows
and columns of type easy.

First, draw an ordinary box. It should be large enough to contain all of the rows or columns
you want to create. Next, select Rows and Columns from the Type menu (see Figure 14.10).
You are presented with the Rows and Columns dialog box (see Figure 14.11). Simply enter

14

the number of rows (horizontal) and columns (vertical) and the gutter (the space between each row or column). The height and width are adjusted automatically. If you have the Preview button checked, you can see the rows and columns changing in real time as you enter the numbers (see Figure 14.12).

Figure 14.10.

Choosing Rows and Columns from the Type menu.

Figure 14.11.

The Rows and Columns dialog box.

Figure 14.12.

The box before and after Rows and Columns has been applied.

To make life even easier, the Rows and Columns feature even links the boxes for you so that type automatically runs from one to the next (see Figure 14.13). By choosing from the Text Flow icons you can specify which direction the type should flow (see Figure 14.14). You can also choose to add guides, which is a great time-saving feature in itself.

14

Figure 14.13.

After the columns are created, the text is placed in the first box, and runs its course through the linked boxes.

Lorem ipsum dolor sit amet, consectetuer adipiscing elit, sed diam nonummy nibh euismod tincidunt ut laoreet dolore magna aliquam erat volutpat. Ut wisi enim ad minim veniam, quis nostrud exerci tation ullamcorper suscipit

lobortis nisl ut aliquip ex ea commodo consequat. Duis autem vel eum iriure dolor in hendrerit in vulputate velit esse molestie consequat, vel illum dolore eu feugiat nulla facilisis at vero eros et accumsan et iusto odio dignissim qui blandit

praesent luptatum zzril delenit augue duis dolore te feugait nulla facilisi. Lorem ipsum dolor sit amet, consectetuer adipiscing elit, sed diam nonummy nibh euismod tincidunt ut laoreet dolore magna aliquam erat volutpat.

Ut wisi enim ad minim veniam, quis nostrud exerci tation ullamcorper suscipit lobortis nisl ut aliquip ex ea commodo consequat. Duis autem vel eum iriure dolor in hendrerit in vulputate velit esse molestie consequat, vel

illum dolore eu feugiat nulla facilisis at vero eros et accumsan et iusto odio dignissim qui blandit praesent luptatum zzril delenit augue duis dolore te feugait nulla facilisi. Nam liber tempor cum soluta nobis eleifend option congue nihil

imperdiet doming id quod mazim placerat facer possim assum. Lorem ipsum dolor sit amet, consectetuer adipiscing elit, sed diam nonummy nibh euismod tincidunt ut laoreet dolore magna aliquam erat volutpat. Ut wisi enim ad minim

Figure 14.14.

These icons specify which way the text should link from box to box.

Now I'll tell you a little secret: You don't have to use Rows and Columns for just text blocks. It's great for making quick grids or rows of even boxes, too!

Type on a Path

One of Illustrator's most popular type features is its capability to place type along a path (see Figure 14.15). You can place text along any path in Illustrator, whether it's an open path or a closed one.

To place text on a path, do one of the following:

☐ With the Path Type tool selected, click any path (see Figure 14.16).

☐ With the Type tool or the Area Type tool selected, click and hold the (Option)[Alt] key while clicking any path. Notice that the cursor changes to the Path Type tool icon when you press the (Option)[Alt] key (see Figure 14.17).

Figure 14.15.

Type on a path.

Figure 14.16.

Choosing the Path Type tool.

Figure 14.17.

With the Type tool selected, the icon changes to the Path Type tool when the (Option)[Alt] key is pressed.

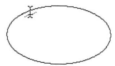

Moving Text Along a Path

When type is on a path, you can move its position as well as flip it to the other side of the path. First, select the type or the path using the Selection tool (the Direct Selection tool or Group Selection tool do not help here). Notice that the path is highlighted as well as the I-beam insertion point for the type. To edit where the type lies on the path, click the I-beam and drag

14

in the direction you want to move the type. To flip the type to the other side of the path, double-click directly on the I-beam or drag towards the opposite side of the path (see Figure 14.18).

Figure 14.18.

By double-clicking the I-beam, you can flip the type to the inside of the circle.

Vertical Text

Illustrator 7 also supports vertical text (see Figure 14.19), as well as complicated alphabets such as Kanji (Japanese). The Vertical Type tool, Vertical Area Type tool, and Vertical Path Type tool all work the same as their horizontal counterparts.

Figure 14.19.

Samples of type created with the vertical text tools.

14

Summary

Up to this point, we've covered just about all the creation tools in Illustrator. First we covered drawing shapes, and now we know how to add text to our illustrations. We learned about the three types of text in Illustrator: point text, area text, and text on a path. But don't go anywhere just yet. There's still plenty more, and next hour we discuss how to work with the text we just learned to create.

Term Review

Point Type—Type in Illustrator that is defined by a single point. Usually used for headlines and logos.

Area Type—Type in Illustrator that is defined by an enclosed shape. Usually used for running body copy.

14

Hour 15

Advanced Typography

In the last hour we learned all about creating text in Illustrator. We learned about the three kinds of text, and we learned how to move the text around. But there's a lot more to text than just the words themselves. In this hour we learn how to work with the type—or more importantly, how to make it look good. Of course, that's our goal with anything we do, and Illustrator has the tools to make text look great. In this hour we learn all about:

- ☐ The Character palette
- ☐ Fonts
- ☐ The Paragraph palette
- ☐ Multiple master fonts

The Character Palette

You control your type (and believe me, type needs *lots* of controlling) using Illustrator's Character palette (see Figure 15.1). In this palette, you specify fonts, point size, leading, and kerning. The Character palette is the central location for editing type style: how your type looks.

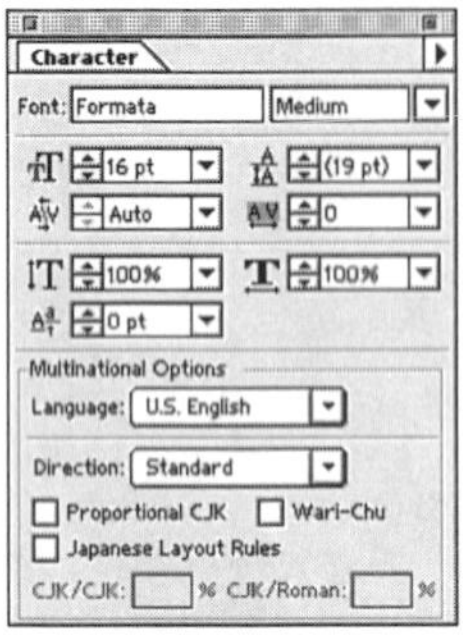

Figure 15.1.
The Character palette, in all its glory, with the Options and Multinational sections open.

To edit type, you must select it. To do so, you can either use the Selection tool to select the entire text block, or you can select type individually by:

☐ Clicking and dragging text with the Type tool

☐ Clicking in the text with the Type tool and pressing the left or right arrow keys on the keyboard while holding down the Shift key

Font

A font is a style of type, usually grouped in families such as Helvetica or Times. There are many different fonts available, and a font is basically the personality of your type. Loud text such as "SALE!" might be in a fat bold font, and more delicate words, such as *love*, might be in a script italic font (see Figure 15.2).

Figure 15.2.
Type in different fonts.

SALE!
Love

After you choose a font, you also specify what style you want, such as Roman (normal), Italic, or Bold, and so on.

Size

Type is traditionally measured in points. You can specify your type to be any size from 0.1 point (*really* small) up to 1296 points (*really* large). You can quickly enlarge or reduce your type in two-point increments by pressing (Command-Shift->)[Control-Shift->] or

15

(Command-Shift-<)[Control-Shift-<], respectively. This works regardless of how you selected the type (with the arrow or the Text tool).

TIME SAVER

> Of course, if you need even bigger type, you can simply convert your text to outlines (we get to that later in this hour). Once your type is a vector object, you can scale to virtually any size with the Scale tool.

Leading

Leading (pronounced *ledding*) is the amount of space between each baseline in a paragraph of type. Leading is also measured in points. If the leading size and the point size are the same, it is called *solid leading*. A lot of space between each baseline is called *open leading*, whereas very little space is called *tight leading* (see Figure 15.3). Leading is important in determining readability. Typically, the wider your block of text, the more leading you need.

Figure 15.3.

Text with open leading (left), and tight leading (right).

AS HARRY CHAPIN

SANG, "ALL MY LIFE'S

A CIRCLE, SUNRISE

AND SUNDOWN. THE

MOON ROLLS

THROUGH THE

NIGHTTIME, TILL THE

DAYBREAK COMES

AROUND...

AS HARRY CHAPIN SANG, "ALL MY LIFE'S A CIRCLE, SUNRISE AND SUNDOWN. THE MOON ROLLS THROUGH THE NIGHTTIME, TILL THE DAYBREAK COMES AROUND...

The keyboard shortcut for increasing and decreasing leading is (Option-up arrow)[Alt-up arrow] and (Option-down arrow)[Alt-down arrow], respectively.

Kerning and Tracking

Kerning is the space between individual letters. Tracking is the amount of letterspacing applied globally across an entire word. Negative numbers mean your kerning or tracking is tight, and the letters are closer to each other. Positive numbers mean your kerning or tracking is loose, and the letters are further apart from each other (see Figure 15.4).

Figure 15.4.
The top word has tight tracking, whereas the bottom type has loose tracking.

KATI

K A T I

The keyboard shortcut for tightening and loosening kerning or tracking is (Option-left arrow)[Alt-left arrow] and (Option-right arrow)[Alt-right arrow], respectively. If you have a word selected, Illustrator automatically applies tracking. Otherwise, invoking the keyboard shortcut applies kerning.

Horizontal and Vertical Scale

Using horizontal and vertical scale, you can adjust the width and height of selected text (see Figure 15.5). This can result in type that looks squashed and can distort text in unsightful ways. For true horizontal and vertical scaling, try to use multiple master typefaces, which are covered later in this chapter.

Figure 15.5.
From the left, the original letter, scaled vertically 50% and then scaled horizontally 50%.

a a a

Baseline Shift

All type is aligned to a baseline. You can select type and shift the baseline for that selection (see Figure 15.6). This is useful for creating superscripts or subscripts and also for creating type effects. But in Illustrator, one of the most useful applications for baseline shift is when you have type on a path (see Figure 15.7). You can use baseline shift to move the type up off the path, and you can give the path a stroke (make sure you use the Direct Selection tool, or the type gets a stroke, too).

Figure 15.6.
The "T" has a positive baseline shift.

KAT I

15

Figure 15.7.

By using baseline shift to move the type up, you can create a colored stroke using the same path the type is on.

15

The keyboard shortcut for raising and lowering baseline shift is (Option-Shift-up arrow) [Alt-Shift-up arrow] and (Option-Shift-down arrow)[Alt-Shift-down arrow], respectively.

The Paragraph Palette

The Paragraph palette is where you specify justification, indents, word and letter spacing, as well as options such as auto-hyphenation and hanging punctuation (see Figure 15.8).

Figure 15.8.

The Paragraph palette.

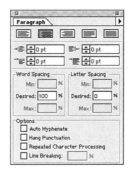

Justification

Justification is a fancy word for paragraph alignment (see Figure 15.9). You can align a paragraph of type in five different ways in Illustrator:

- ☐ Flush left
- ☐ Flush right

☐ Centered

☐ Justified

☐ Forced justified (flush left *and* right)

You can select these quickly by clicking the icons found at the top of the Paragraph palette (see Figure 15.10).

Figure 15.9.

Paragraph alignment.

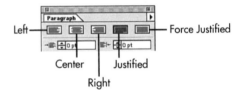

Figure 15.10.

The justification icons in the Paragraph palette.

The keyboard shortcuts for justification are as follows:

☐ **Left:** (Command-Shift-L)[Control-Shift-L]

☐ **Right:** (Command-Shift-R)[Control-Shift-R]

☐ **Center:** (Command-Shift-C)[Control-Shift-C]

☐ **Justified:** (Command-Shift-J)[Control-Shift-J]

☐ **Forced Justified:** (Command-Shift-F)[Control-Shift-F]

JUST A MINUTE

For some reason, Adobe assigned the (Command-Shift-L)[Control-Shift-L] keyboard shortcut to two different functions: unlocking objects and making type flush left. Unlocking objects takes precedence, so if you have a locked item on your page, and you attempt to make text flush left by using the keyboard shortcut, Illustrator first unlocks the art. You then need to reselect the text and run the shortcut again.

Indents

There are three different indent settings: Left Indent, First Line Indent, and Right Indent. The left and right indents affect the entire paragraph of type, whereas the first line indents from the left on the first line of the paragraph.

15

There is also a setting for space before each paragraph. Sometimes you want to add a little bit of extra space before each paragraph to increase readability, as well as make it easier to identify where a paragraph ends and the next one begins (see Figure 15.11).

Figure 15.11.

The different paragraph settings.

LEFT INDENT	FIRST LINE INDENT	RIGHT INDENT	SPACE BEFORE PARAGRAPH
Lorem ipsum dolor sit amet, consectetuer adipiscing elit, sed diam nonummy nibh euismod tincidunt ut laoreet dolore magna aliquam erat volutpat. Ut wisi enim ad minim veniam, quis nostrud exerci tation ullamcorper suscipit lobortis nisl ut aliquip ex ea commodo consequat. Duis autem vel eum iriure dolor in hendrerit in vulputate velit esse molestie consequat, vel	Lorem ipsum dolor sit amet, consectetuer adipiscing elit, sed diam nonummy nibh euismod tincidunt ut laoreet dolore magna aliquam erat volutpat. Ut wisi enim ad minim veniam, quis nostrud exerci tation ullamcorper suscipit lobortis nisl ut aliquip ex ea commodo consequat. Duis autem vel eum iriure dolor in hendrerit in vulputate velit esse molestie consequat, vel illum dolore	Lorem ipsum dolor sit amet, consectetuer adipiscing elit, sed diam nonummy nibh euismod tincidunt ut laoreet dolore magna aliquam erat volutpat. Ut wisi enim ad minim veniam, quis nostrud exerci tation ullamcorper suscipit lobortis nisl ut aliquip ex ea commodo consequat. Duis autem vel eum iriure dolor in hendrerit in vulputate velit esse molestie consequat, vel	Lorem ipsum dolor sit amet, consectetuer adipiscing elit, sed diam nonummy nibh euismod tincidunt ut laoreet dolore magna aliquam erat volutpat. Ut wisi enim ad minim veniam, quis nostrud exerci tation ullamcorper suscipit lobortis nisl ut aliquip ex ea commodo consequat. Duis autem vel eum iriure dolor in hendrerit in

Word and Letter Spacing

These settings let you control spacing between words and letters when justified or forced justified type is used. These settings control when words become hyphenated, or forced to another line, by specifying how far Illustrator can stretch the spacing between words and letters.

The Tab Palette

To create tabs in a paragraph, open the Tab Ruler by choosing it from the Type menu (see Figure 15.12). It's a floating palette, so you can position it anywhere on the page (see Figure 15.13). To add a tab, click the ruler where you want the tab to be. After you click, a highlighted tab arrow appears. You can now make the tab a right, center, left, or decimal tab by clicking the icons in the upper-left corner of the Tab palette (see Figure 15.14). To delete a tab, drag it off the palette (see Figure 15.15), and to quickly change the measurement system, Shift-click in the upper portion of the palette.

Figure 15.12.

Choosing the Tab palette from the Type menu.

Figure 15.13.

The Tab palette.

Figure 15.14.
*Clicking these icons
defines the type of tab.*

Figure 15.15.
Deleting a tab.

The MM Design Palette

Illustrator 7 has full support for multiple master typefaces. Developed by Adobe, a multiple master typeface contains a variable width or weight or even serif axis (see Figure 15.16). By controlling the axis, you can modify the typeface to fit your exact specifications. The MM Design palette lets you modify multiple master typefaces in real time right in Illustrator (see Figure 15.17). Simply drag the sliders to edit the typeface. You need to have a Multiple Master font to use this feature.

Figure 15.16.
*A multiple master
typeface can have scalable
widths or weights.*

Figure 15.17.
The MM Design palette.

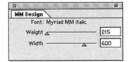

Converting Text to Outlines

One of the most powerful text features in Illustrator is the ability to convert type into fully editable Bézier paths. By choosing Create Outlines (see Figure 15.18) from the Type menu (you need to have type selected with the Selection tool when you do this), Illustrator turns the type into Bézier paths. You can then edit each individual letter using the techniques we learned in previous chapters (see Figure 15.19). You can even use the type as a mask.

Figure 15.18.

Choosing Create Outlines from the Type menu (Command-Shift O) [Control-Shift-O].

Figure 15.19.

Editing type that was converted to outlines.

There are two other reasons why you would want to convert type to outlines. One is that certain plug-in filters don't work on type. So to run those filters, you need to convert your type to outlines first. Another reason is if you are sending your file out to another person, or to your service bureau, who might not have your font. Converting the type to outlines assures it will print perfectly. When you create a logo, it's always a good idea to convert any type to outlines. This way whenever you use it, you don't have to worry about fonts.

TIME SAVER

After text is converted to curves, it cannot be turned back into text again, so you can't fix any typos. It might be a good idea to save a version of your file before you convert your text to curves, in case you need to edit the text.

Change Case

It happens all the time: you type something all in caps, and you need it in lowercase, or vice versa. Well, with this handy little feature, your hands are spared a few more moments from that repetitive strain injury. Simply highlight the type with the Type tool and choose Change Case from the Type menu (see Figure 15.20). You can then choose how you want your type changed (see Figure 15.21).

Figure 15.20.

Choosing Change Case from the Type menu.

Figure 15.21.

The Change Case dialog box.

Find Font and Find/Change

You just finished an entire job and the client calls to say they loved it, but could you just change one little thing? They want all instances of the word Fred to be changed to Frederick, and in a different typeface. After you hang up the phone and slam your head into the monitor, go to the Type menu and select Find Font (see Figure 15.22). Here you can easily change one font to another throughout the document (see Figure 15.23). As far as changing the actual text, select Find/Change from the Type menu and in the Find/Change dialog box (see Figure 15.24), type in what word you are looking for, and what it should be changed to. These functions work the same as they would in any word processing program. All happy now?

Figure 15.22.

Selecting Find Font from the Type menu.

15

Figure 15.23.
The Find Font dialog box.

Figure 15.24.
The Find/Change dialog box.

Smart Punctuation

If you want to make your type look as if it were set by an expert typographer, use Smart Punctuation (see Figure 15.25). It replaces regular quotes with the curly kind (see Figure 15.26) and inserts ligatures, em and en dashes, ellipses, and expert fractions in your document.

Figure 15.25.
Found in the Type menu, the Smart Punctuation feature lets you make changes to selected text or an entire document.

Figure 15.26.
From left to right, plain quotes, and curly quotes.

Check Spelling

Illustrator also has a built-in spell checker (see Figure 15.27). It works like any other spell checker you would find in a word processor. You can find it in the Type menu (see Figure 15.28).

Figure 15.27.
*Choosing Check Spelling
from the Type menu.*

Figure 15.28.
*Illustrator's Check
Spelling dialog box.*

Summary

Fonts, points, leading, kerning, indents, justification: We learned all about these fancy words
this hour along with a lot of other cool stuff. We learned how to use Multiple Master fonts
as well as how to adjust word and letter spacing. The Change Case filter will save us many
hours of extra typing, and we really felt the power of Illustrator when we converted type to
outlines and edited the Bézier paths. By the way, converting type to paths and analyzing how
the points are set up is a good way to learn more about Bézier paths.

15

Term Review

15

Fonts—Typestyles of different varieties, such as serif, sans serif, and script.

Points—Measurement system used for measuring type. There are 72 points in one inch, and there are 12 points in a Pica.

Leading—The amount of space between lines of type (pronounced ledding).

Kerning—The process of adding or removing space between letters.

Indents—Term used to indicate shortening or lengthening the width of a paragraph.

Justification—Term used to describe the alignment of the text in a paragraph—Left, Right, and so on.

Multiple Master—A font technology developed by Adobe Systems that gives a font the capability to be scaled on either a weight, width, or serif axis.

Hour **16**

Working with Raster Images

Way back in Hour 1, we discussed the differences between vector and raster images. To quickly review, vector images are mathematically defined (Bézier) shapes that can be scaled to virtually any size without any loss in detail. Raster images are defined by individual pixels, which combine to create an image. Raster images, however, are bound by the resolution in which they were created, and scaling pixel images can produce jaggy or unclear results (see Figure 16.1). Although it is a vector program, Illustrator does have support for raster art. In this hour, we learn about:

- ☐ Placing raster images
- ☐ Linking and embedding
- ☐ Working with raster art in Illustrator

Figure 16.1.

Both have been enlarged 300%. Notice how the raster image becomes jaggy, whereas the vector image remains smooth.

A Pixel for Your Thoughts

There are basically two ways to get a raster image into Illustrator. The first way is to place the image. This command takes an existing raster image and places it into your document. The second way is to convert a vector object into a raster object by using Illustrator's Rasterize command. There is a really a third way—opening a raster file directly—but we'll get to that later in the chapter.

Placing an Image

If you've used any page layout program, either PageMaker or QuarkXPress, you're familiar with the Place command. Place lets you import an image right into your Illustrator document. The image could either have been created in another application or it could have been exported from Illustrator in a raster format (see Hour 20, "Saving/Exporting Files").

To place a raster image, choose Place from the File menu (see Figure 16.2). You are then prompted with a dialog box asking you to find the file you want to place. After selecting the file, click Place. The image appears in the center of your screen (see Figure 16.3).

Figure 16.2.

Choosing Place from the File menu.

Figure 16.3.

The placed EPS file.

16

Notice that the image has a box with an "x" through it that shows the image is selected. Note that the "x" appears only on linked EPS images. All other placed images, whether linked or embedded, have just a box surrounding the image. You can only view placed images when in Preview mode. When you are in Artwork mode, you only see the surrounding box, not the image. EPS files are the one exception to this rule. In the View section of the Document Setup dialog box, there is a Show Placed EPS Artwork option that enables you to see a low resolution black and white preview of the EPS image when in Artwork mode.

The Rasterize Command

Any object in Illustrator can be rasterized right inside Illustrator using the Rasterize command. Essentially, you are instructing Illustrator to convert a vector object into a raster. When an image is rasterized it becomes an embedded image (see "Linked and Embedded Images" later in this chapter).

1. Select one or more objects.
2. Choose Rasterize from the Object menu (see Figure 16.4).

Figure 16.4.

The Rasterize dialog box.

3. Choose a color model. You can select either RGB, CMYK, Grayscale, or Bitmap.
4. Next, choose a resolution. When Illustrator converts your selection to pixels, it needs to know how many pixels to create. For screen and web art, choose 72 dpi. If your art will be printed on an imagesetter, you need higher resolution—closer to 300 dpi for photographic images; 600 or more for bitmap and line art.
5. Finally, choose whether you want anti-aliasing or a mask. Both of these features are described in detail later in this chapter.

TIME SAVER

Everyone knows that you can use the Rasterize command on vector objects, but did you know that you can also apply the Rasterize command to raster art? This is most useful for converting color images to grayscale (select Grayscale from the Color Model pop-up menu) or for converting grayscale images into color (some Photoshop-compatible filters work only on RGB images).

Anti-aliasing

One of the biggest advantages of vector art is the smooth lines you get when you print the file. Today's high-end imagesetters print at resolutions upwards of 2500 dpi, and we are used to seeing the clean sharp edges in our logos, type, and illustrations. Onscreen, however, things can appear jaggy because a monitor's resolution is only 72 dpi.

When your final art is printed, the images will be ultra-sharp, but what if your images *won't* be printed? What if you are designing for the Web or for a multimedia presentation, and the final art will be viewed onscreen? Do we have to live with jaggy art in these situations? That's where anti-aliasing comes in.

Anti-aliasing is the process of slightly blurring the edges of an image to give it a softer, smoother edge onscreen. Adobe's ATM (Adobe Type Manager) uses this technology to enable fonts to appear smooth onscreen at any size (see the following Just a Minute). Almost all images on the Web use anti-aliasing to give a clean and smooth appearance.

JUST A MINUTE

You may notice that when in Preview mode, all type appears anti-aliased (assuming you enabled the Anti-alias Type option in the Keyboard Increments screen of the Preferences dialog box). When you switch to Artwork mode, the type is not anti-aliased. This anti-aliasing appears only onscreen, however—when you print the file, you still get the sharp lines you are used to. This is a great feature that Adobe added as of version 7. Of course, after you convert text to outlines, it does not appear anti-aliased onscreen.

When you use the Rasterize command to convert a vector object to raster, and the final image will appear onscreen at 72 dpi, anti-alias the object to give it that smooth appearance. To do so, simply check the Anti-Alias checkbox in the Rasterize dialog box (see Figure 16.5)

Figure 16.5.

Checking the Anti-Alias box when invoking the Rasterize command ensures smooth edges.

Creating a Mask

A raster image always has a rectangular-shaped bounding box that defines the area of the image. Although vector files can have irregularly shaped edges, a raster requires a clipping path to achieve a different shaped border. When you rasterize an object in Illustrator, you have the option to create a mask for the image (see Figure 16.6). This allows you to place the rasterized image on a colored background without the white background box filling in around the rasterized art (see Figure 16.7).

Figure 16.6.

Checking the Create Mask checkbox when invoking the Rasterize command.

Figure 16.7.

The raster image on the left has no mask, whereas the raster image on the right was created using the Create Mask option.

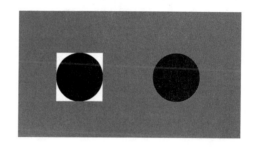

To create a mask for an object at the time you rasterize it, simply check the Create Mask button in the Rasterize dialog box.

Opening an Image

I mentioned earlier that there is a third way to bring a pixel image into Illustrator. Besides placing a file or using the Rasterize command, you can also use the Open command to directly open a raster image, which creates a new document with the raster image in it. Remember, however, that when you open a raster file, it automatically becomes embedded in the Illustrator document, and you cannot link it.

Illustrator 7 also sports a brand new and improved EPS parser. This means you can open just about any vector EPS (Encapsulated PostScript) file and edit it as if it were an Illustrator document. You can save a QuarkXPress document as an EPS, for example, and then open the file (not place it) and edit the document. It should be noted, however, that editing text may be difficult due to the way the text is imported.

JUST A MINUTE

The EPS format, unlike any other, can support both raster and vector art—even within the same document. The parser in Illustrator can only convert vector EPS images (or the vector parts within an EPS) into editable art. Any art that is in raster format remains in raster form and can be edited only as a raster image.

Linked and Embedded Images

As if things weren't already complicated enough, there are two ways Illustrator handles raster images. A raster image can either be *linked*, or *embedded* in an Illustrator document. Except for certain file formats, Illustrator links placed images by default.

A linked file resides outside of your Illustrator file, and Illustrator notes the location of that file, be it on your hard drive, on a Zip disk, or on a file server. The image in your document is simply a preview of that raster file. At print time, Illustrator goes to the original file and uses the high resolution information to print the image where it belongs in the illustration. You cannot print your file without that original raster image.

An embedded raster is actually part of your Illustrator document. After you embed a raster file, you no longer need the original raster file because the entire image is contained within your Illustrator document. Of course, this also means that your file size increases (if the file is a high-resolution one, your Illustrator file could grow to be extremely large).

If you decide not to link a file when you place it, uncheck Link when you import it (see Figure 16.8). The image will then be embedded.

Figure 16.8.

Unchecking the Link box in the Place dialog box.

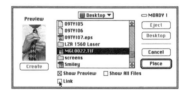

TIME SAVER

If you have a linked image in a file, and then you delete or remove the linked image from its directory, Illustrator can't access the image anymore. The next time you open the file, Illustrator alerts you and asks you where the file currently is. If you can't find it, Illustrator opens the document without the image in place.

File Formats

Illustrator 7 supports a wide range of image formats. Depending on which platform you are using, Macintosh or Windows, you can open and place an array of different file formats. Some are specific to one particular program and others are specific to either the Macintosh or Windows platform, such as PICT and BMP.

There are, however, formats that can be used on either the Macintosh or Windows platforms. These formats include native Illustrator files, Acrobat PDF, TIFF, and EPS formats. PDF files can be viewed on any platform (even the World Wide Web) with the Acrobat Reader program.

16

Color Management

Illustrator 7 sports a robust color management system that works in conjunction with either Apple ColorSync (Macintosh) or the Kodak Digital Science Color Management System (Windows). These are installed when you install Illustrator. You can edit the color settings in Illustrator by choosing Color Settings from the File menu (see Figure 16.9). You can fine-tune your options within the Color Settings dialog box (see Figure 16.10).

Figure 16.9.

Choosing Color Settings from the File menu.

Figure 16.10.

The Color Settings dialog box.

A color management system strives to keep colors consistent as you work with them—from scanning, to viewing onscreen, to proofing, to final output. Because each of these processes use different color technologies and even different color models, there can be a noticeable difference from what you see onscreen and what you actually get when the job is printed. Technologies such as ColorSync and Kodak Digital Science compensate for color differences by using color profiles from each device, such as your scanner, monitor, and printer, and try to make color consistent across the board.

A great feature of Illustrator is the ability to simulate print colors on display. This option lets you view files just like in Photoshop, when you want to view only certain color channels. It's also great when doing print work to get a better idea of how your file is going to print.

Notice also the checkbox marked Use ICC profiles with TIFF. With this option enabled (which it is by default), when you place a TIFF image, Illustrator prompts you with a dialog box to help calibrate the colors onscreen, making for more accurate color representation onscreen (see Figure 16.11). Of course, you can choose to leave everything as it is by clicking the Ignore Profile button.

Figure 16.11.

The TIFF Color
Management Options
dialog box pops up when
you place a TIFF file.

What Can I Do with Raster Art in Illustrator?

Placed raster images cannot be edited in Illustrator. You can, however, apply transformations to them, and you can also apply certain filters. You transform raster images just as you would any Illustrator object: select it and apply the transformation. This applies to all the transformation commands and tools—moving, scaling, rotating, reflecting, and shearing.

Colorize 1-bit TIFFs

Illustrator has the capability to colorize 1-bit (black and white) TIFF images. After placing the image into your document, you can assign one color to the black part of the image by assigning a fill to the image.

Use the Autotrace Tool

One of the reasons why you would place a raster image into Illustrator is to trace it. Tracing a raster image creates a vector object that you can edit and scale without worrying about resolution. Illustrator's Autotrace tool was created with this in mind.

1. Place a raster image into your Illustrator document.
2. Choose the Autotrace tool from the Toolbox.
3. Click the edge of the image to trace.

The Curve Fitting Tolerance setting in Preferences determines how close and how smooth the traced object is in reference to the raster image. If you need more detail and accuracy for your tracing, you might look into Adobe Streamline, a software product geared specifically towards converting raster to vector art. For more information on tracing images, see Hour 21, "Working Smart in Illustrator."

Use Photoshop-Compatible Filters

Finally, one of the most exciting things you can do to raster images in Illustrator is apply Photoshop-compatible filters to them. Illustrator ships with several filters, including the entire Gallery Effects library of Photoshop-compatible filters. To use a filter, it must be present in Illustrator's Plug-ins folder when you launch Illustrator.

16

Photoshop-compatible filters can only be run on embedded raster images, not linked ones. Also, many Photoshop-compatible filters work only on images that are in RGB color mode. If you have an image that is not RGB, use the Rasterize command to convert to the RGB color space.

Photoshop-compatible filters can be found under the Filter menu. They look just like the other filters, but they are grayed-out unless you have an embedded raster image selected (see Figure 16.12).

Figure 16.12.

Without an embedded raster image selected, all Photoshop-compatible filters are grayed out.

Have fun with the filters, and remember that you can always use the Rasterize command to convert vector art into a raster image, enabling you to apply Photoshop-compatible filters to it.

For more information on Photoshop-compatible filters, check out either *Illustrator 7 Complete* or *Photoshop 4 Complete*. These books do a great job of reviewing the filters, their settings, and the results you get.

Summary

Well, we learned to live with our pixel friends, and we proved that raster and vector images can coexist peacefully. We learned about linking and embedding, and also about Illustrator's powerful EPS parser. As if that weren't enough, we traced pixel images and even applied Photoshop-compatible filters to rasters within Illustrator. Next, we get back to the world of vector images and explore all of the filters we can apply to vector objects.

Term Review

Color management—Software on a system level, such as Apple's ColorSync or Kodak's Digital Science, that assures consistent color on screens, scanners, printers and imagesetters.

Link—An external raster file that is referenced from within an Illustrator document.

Embed—A raster image that has been included within an Illustrator document.

Place—The act of importing an image or art into an Illustrator document.

1-bit—A raster image that contains only black and white pixels.

16

Hour 17

Vector Filters

Illustrator filters, found in the Filter menu (see Figure 17.1), perform a wide variety of tasks, ranging from simple time-savers such as converting all colors to CMYK to more complex functions such as creating intricate borders using the Path Patterns filter. In this hour, we focus on some of these filters, including

- ☐ The Adjust Colors filter
- ☐ The Object Mosaic filter
- ☐ The Roughen filter
- ☐ The Twirl filter
- ☐ The Zig Zag filter

Figure 17.1.

The Illustrator Filter
menu.

The Filter Menu

The Filter menu actually started out as a place for Illustrator plug-ins, but now that plug-ins can appear anywhere within Illustrator, the Filter menu has become the dumping ground for functions that don't really belong under any other menu. If you have any third-party plug-ins installed, such as KPT Vector Effects or Extensis VectorTools, you'll find them in the Filter menu. So if you have some filters that are not covered in this chapter, please refer to the documentation that came with those filters. For more information on plug-ins, see Hour 21, "Working Smart in Illustrator."

I've broken down the filters as they appear in the Filter menu, and they fall under the following categories: Color, Creation, and Distortion. The rest are Photoshop-compatible filters that apply to raster objects only.

Before we begin, at the top of the Filter menu, you'll notice two commands: Apply Last Filter and Last Filter. These can be used to quickly invoke the last filter you used. The Apply Last Filter option runs the last filter you used, with the settings you used. The Last Filter option opens the dialog box of the last filter you ran, enabling you to adjust the settings before running the filter. Remember the keystrokes ((Command-E)[Control-E] and (Command-Option-E)[Control-Alt-E], respectively) for these two commands, as there are times when you may want to use a filter repeatedly.

Color Filters

The Color filters are production-based filters that you use to fine-tune colors as well as to address color issues to prepare files for film output (see Figure 17.2).

Figure 17.2.

The Colors filters.

JUST A MINUTE

It's important to point out that these filters do not work on objects filled with gradients or patterns. If you want to adjust them with these filters, you have to convert them into art using the Expand function (refer to Hour 6, "Drawing Bézier Paths," for detailed information on the Expand command).

Adjust Colors

The Adjust Colors filter lets you tweak the colors of an object or a group of objects (see Figure 17.3). Similar to Photoshop's Levels command, you can adjust colors by changing the CMYK, Grayscale, or RGB values. You can adjust either just the fill, the stroke, or both simultaneously and preview your results as well (although this may slow down performance). You can even click the Convert button to change all selected objects to your current color mode, indicated in the pop-up menu at the top of the Adjust Colors dialog box.

Figure 17.3.

The Adjust Colors dialog box.

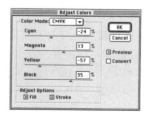

Blending Objects

These three filters, Blend Front to Back, Blend Horizontally, and Blend Vertically, do not affect the objects (as the Blend tool does) but affect the fill color within them. You must have at least three objects selected for these filters to work. Upon running the filter, Illustrator blends the color across the selected objects (see Figure 17.4).

Figure 17.4.
After you run the Blend Horizontally filter on the row of circles on top, the color is blended evenly across the circles, as shown on bottom.

Switching Between Color Models

These filters—Convert to CMYK, Convert to Grayscale, and Convert to RGB—speak for themselves. When used, any item selected is converted to the color mode chosen. Remember that these filters do *not* convert gradients or patterns.

Inverting Colors

The Invert Colors filter, identical to the one found in Photoshop, creates an inverted color (negative) for the selected objects.

Merge Spot Colors

This filter is important when preparing spot color jobs for film output. Illustrator enables you to create multiple spot colors with the same swatch name. This may present problems when sending out for film separations because if you have several swatches named "red," how will Illustrator know which one to use? Running the Merge Spot Colors filter checks your document for spot colors with the same name and deletes duplicate swatches, leaving you with only one swatch for each color.

Overprint Black

On most print jobs, you may need to set the black ink to overprint (as opposed to *knockout*, where the top color prints, but the color behind it does not). For simple jobs that require trapping, overprinting the black ink solves most trapping problems. Instead of having to select each object individually, and then choosing the Overprint option in the Attributes palette, simply running the Overprint Black filter saves a lot of time (see Figure 17.5). Refer to Hour 13, "The Pathfinder Commands," for more information on overprinting and trapping.

Figure 17.5.
The Overprint Black filter's dialog box.

17

Saturate

The Saturate filter can be a lot of fun (see Figure 17.6). Using a simple slider, you can saturate or desaturate the color in an object or a group of objects. This filter is great for creating subtle changes in color as well as making certain objects more or less vibrant than other objects.

Figure 17.6.
The Saturate filter's
dialog box.

Create Filters

Basically time-savers, the Create filters let you do in one step what might normally take a lot more (see Figure 17.7). You'll also find the Object Mosaic filter here, a powerful filter that can be used to create really interesting effects.

Figure 17.7.
Illustrator's Create filter
menu.

Fill & Stroke for Mask

When you create a mask, the object that is the mask cannot have any fill or stroke attributes. But sometimes you'd like the mask to have a stroke or fill. With the mask selected, running the Fill & Stroke for Mask filter applies a fill and stroke to the mask based on what the mask attributes were before the mask was created.

In other words, if you used a square with a 1 point black rule and a yellow fill to make a mask, running the filter applies those attributes to the mask. The way Illustrator accomplishes this is by creating a new square with a fill of yellow and a new square with a stroke of black and a fill of None and then sending them to the back and front of the mask, respectively.

Although you could actually do this manually, with the filter you can do it in one step.

Object Mosaic

Object Mosaic is a powerful filter used to create a vector tile-like mosaic based on a raster image (see Figure 17.8).

Figure 17.8.

The image on the left is the original raster. The image on the right is the mosaic created after running the Object Mosaic filter.

Follow these steps to use the filter:

1. Select a raster image.

2. Choose Filter➥Create Object➥Mosaic (see Figure 17.9).

Figure 17.9.

Choosing the Object Mosaic filter.

3. Set your options in the Object Mosaic dialog box. You can choose to delete the raster image after the filter is run (see Figure 17.10).

Figure 17.10.

Setting the options in the Object Mosaic dialog box.

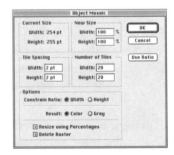

Try different settings to get different results. Remember, you can also run the Object Mosaic filter on objects rasterized in Illustrator with the Rasterize command. Try using Object Mosaic on rasterized type for some cool effects!

17

Trim Marks

This filter creates a set of trim marks (a.k.a. crop marks) around any selected object. Depending on what option you have set in Preferences, Illustrator creates either standard or Japanese style trim marks (see Figure 17.11).

Figure 17.11.

In Preferences, you can choose from either standard (above) or Japanese trim marks (below).

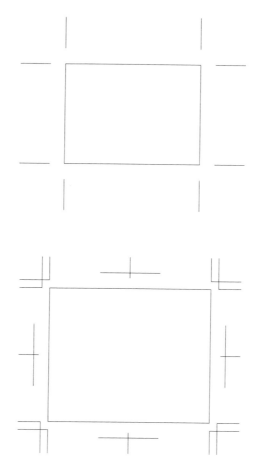

Distortion Filters

For those of you who like to take reality into other dimensions, Illustrator's distort filters will be right up your alley (see Figure 17.12). Whether it's minor tweaking or major funk, these filters comply with the most twisted and demented tasks. Remember that these filters do not work on gradients or patterns, unless you expand them first. (Try it; twirling an expanded gradient is way-cool!)

Figure 17.12.

The Distort filters in the
Filters menu.

Free Distort

For simple, straight distortions, the Free Distort filter lets you edit a selection with four straight points. Dragging each of the points distorts the selection. Clicking the Show Me button previews your distortion in the Free Distort dialog box (see Figure 17.13).

Figure 17.13.

Using the Free Distort
filter.

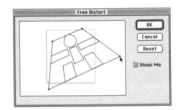

Punk & Bloat

The Punk & Bloat filter, shown in Figure 17.14, does some pretty wild things to art. This filter changes the Bézier curves in a selection to make either sharp points (punk) or round puffy points (bloat), as seen in Figure 17.15.

Figure 17.14.

The Punk & Bloat filter.

17

Figure 17.15.
The original star is in the center. To the left is the "punked" star, to the right, the "bloated" one.

Roughen

Of all the distort filters, Roughen is probably used the most and has some very practical applications (see Figure 17.16). The Roughen filter makes objects appear rough by adding anchor points and moving them around. If you keep the settings really low, you can make your art look almost hand-drawn (see Figure 17.17). The Distort filter is also great for creating torn or crumpled-looking paper.

Figure 17.16.
The Roughen filter.

Figure 17.17.
The original star (left) and what it looks like after the Roughen filter is used (right).

Scribble and Tweak

The Scribble and Tweak filter, shown in Figure 17.18, is difficult to describe. Based on your settings, Scribble randomly moves anchor points away from the original object, whereas Tweak moves anchor points around on the object, creating interesting distortions, to say the least (see Figure 17.19).

Figure 17.18.
The Scribble and Tweak filter dialog box.

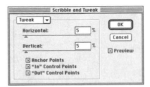

Figure 17.19.
From left to right: the original star, scribbled, and tweaked.

Twirl

The Twirl filter is really cool (see Figure 17.20). The filter actually curves the art in a circular motion from the center, as shown in Figure 17.21, based on the number you enter in the Twirl filter dialog box. If you want to Twirl an object by eye and watch it change in real time, you can use the Twirl tool, which can be found with the Rotate tool (see Figure 17.22). Click and drag with the tool and watch your selection spin before your very eyes!

Figure 17.20.
The Twirl filter dialog box.

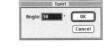

Figure 17.21.
From left to right: the original star, twirled 30°, twirled 100°.

Figure 17.22.
Selecting the Twirl tool from the Toolbox.

Zig Zag

The Zig Zag filter, shown in Figure 17.23, is another distort filter that wreaks havoc on anchor points. Playing with the settings on this one can also produce some wild and interesting results (see Figure 17.24).

Figure 17.23.

The Zig Zag filter dialog box.

Figure 17.24.

On the left is the original star, on the right is...well, your guess is as good as mine.

Summary

So many filters! We covered a lot of ground today discussing all of Illustrator's filters, which enhance our productivity and creativity. You never know when you could use the Roughen filter or even Object Mosaic to add that special touch to your artwork. You're probably wondering about the rest of the filters found in the Filter menu, such as the Ink Pen. Well, hold on to your chair because in the next hour we dive right in to the rest of these filters.

Term Review

Knockout—Term used in trapping to indicate the top color obliterating any color below it.

Hour **18**

Filters with Style

As we all know, style is very important when it comes to working in design. A client always wants a certain style in his design or a certain look and feel. The filters in this chapter can help define a style in your work and help you achieve that look you've been searching for. We've seen that Illustrator's vector filters can do some pretty cool stuff, and in this chapter, we'll see that they can do some pretty powerful stuff as well. This hour covers:

- ☐ The Ink Pen filter
- ☐ Adding arrowheads
- ☐ Path Patterns
- ☐ Photoshop-compatible filters

The Ink Pen

Sometimes people don't get the credit they deserve. And sometimes *filters* don't get the credit they deserve. The Ink Pen filter fits that description perfectly. A powerful filter, the Ink Pen fills objects with complex stippling and crosshatching effects (see Figure 18.1).

Figure 18.1.

Some samples of rect-
angles filled using the Ink
Pen filter.

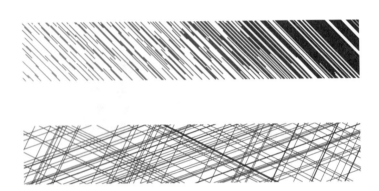

To fill an object with the Ink Pen filter, select the object and choose Filter➡Ink Pen➡Effects (see Figure 18.2). You are then presented with the Ink Pen Effects dialog box (see Figure 18.3), where you can set exactly how you want the effect to look. It should be noted that the Ink Pen filter produces complex fills that may produce large files and may even cause printing problems in some cases.

Figure 18.2.

Choosing Ink Pen Effects.

Figure 18.3.

The Ink Pen Effects
dialog box.

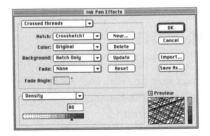

18

You can even create your own hatches for use in the Ink Pen filter. To do so, choose Hatches from the Ink Pen submenu (see Figure 18.4). You are presented with a dialog box where you can import and export hatches (see Figure 18.5).

Figure 18.4.

Choosing Ink Pen Hatches.

Figure 18.5.

The Ink Pen Hatches dialog box.

For more in-depth detail on exactly what each setting does in the Ink Pen dialog boxes, refer to the Adobe Illustrator manual.

Stylize Filters

The Stylize group of filters, shown in Figure 18.6, is used to add unique and interesting effects and accents to art. Some, such as Path Patterns, are extremely powerful; others, such as Add Arrowheads and Round Corners, may not seem so important, but we'll see how they too can be used to save precious time when creating artwork.

Figure 18.6.

The Stylize filters.

Add Arrowheads

You're creating a diagram and you need to create an arrow to point something out in the illustration. No problem. Just draw a line and use the Add Arrowheads filter (see Figure 18.7).

You can apply one of 27 different styles at the beginning, the end, or both ends of the line. The head of the arrow is aligned on the exact same angle as the line, so the arrow is always perfect.

Figure 18.7.

The Add Arrowheads filter's dialog box.

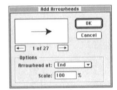

Calligraphy

Looking for that old-fashioned calligraphy style? Look no further. The Calligraphy filter (see Figure 18.8) takes any stroked path and makes it look as if it were drawn with a flat-edged nib—a calligraphy pen (see Figure 18.9). The stroke is converted to a filled path when you run the filter.

Figure 18.8.

The Calligraphy filter dialog box.

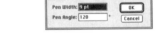

Figure 18.9.

The original image on the left, and the stylized image on the right after running the Calligraphy filter.

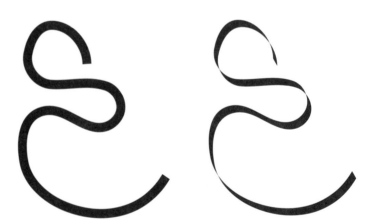

Drop Shadow

The Drop Shadow filter (see Figure 18.10) is, in my opinion, the most useless filter ever devised. The result of running the filter is simply a duplicate of your object offset from the original. First of all, it's ugly, and second of all, it can be created in a fraction of the time by simply (Option-dragging)[Alt-dragging] the shape (copying it) and then pressing (Command-Shift-[)[Control-Shift-[] (send to back).

18

Figure 18.10.

*The Drop Shadow filter
dialog box.*

Path Pattern

Path Patterns are way-cool because instead of having just an ordinary rule or even a dotted line as your border, you can create virtually any artwork to follow a path. Any pattern that you define within Illustrator can be used as a Path Pattern (refer to Hour 6, "Drawing Bézier Paths," for details on defining a pattern).

To apply a Path Pattern, select an object and choose Filter➡Stylize➡Path Pattern (see Figure 18.11). Then choose your settings (see Figure 18.12), click OK, and voilà!

Figure 18.11.

Choosing Path Pattern.

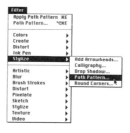

18

Figure 18.12.

*The Path Pattern dialog
box.*

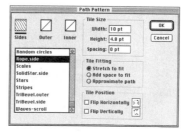

After a Path Pattern is applied, it is no longer a stroke or a pattern. It's actual art that you can edit or color as you want (see Figure 18.13).

Figure 18.13.

*The stroke before and
after the "Rope" Path
Pattern is applied.*

Round Corners

The Round Corners filter, shown in Figure 18.14, didn't appear to be useful to me at first. I mean, if I wanted rounded corners, I would use the Rounded Corner Rectangle tool, right? Then I realized you could apply the Round Corner filter to *any* shape (see Figure 18.15). Sometimes the Round Corners filter can be a real time-saver.

Figure 18.14.
The Round Corners dialog box.

Figure 18.15.
The Round Corners filter gave these road signs just the touch they needed.

Photoshop-compatible Filters

Illustrator ships with many Photoshop-compatible filters (see Figure 18.16), which you can use on any raster image. Refer to Hour 16, "Working with Raster Images," for more information concerning applying these filters.

18

Figure 18.16.

*The lower section of the
Filter menu contains
filters for raster images.*

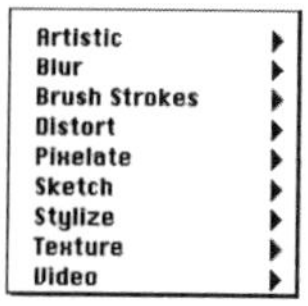

Summary

Today we learned about some pretty cool filters that can help us in our everyday designs, such as the Add Arrowheads filter and the Round Corners filter. We learned all about the Ink Pen filter and how it can help us make fills that look more natural, and we also covered Path Patterns, which allow us to be virtually limitless when it comes to creating complex borders.

18

Hour 19

Charts and Graphs

Presenting data in a graphical manner has an enormous impact. I'm referring of course to graphs or charts used to convey numerical data in a graphical way, making it easier to understand, as well as making it more useful (see Figure 19.1).

The advantage of using Illustrator for graphs over a program such as Harvard Graphics, which is a dedicated graphing program, is that when you create a graph in Illustrator, it is made up of Illustrator vector objects. This means you can edit it just as you would any illustration, giving you complete control over how your graph looks. If necessary, you can then export the graph in any of Illustrator's many export formats. In this hour, we cover:

☐ Creating a graph
☐ Importing graph data
☐ Working with graph designs

Figure 19.1.

Using Illustrator's powerful features, you can produce eye-catching charts such as this one.

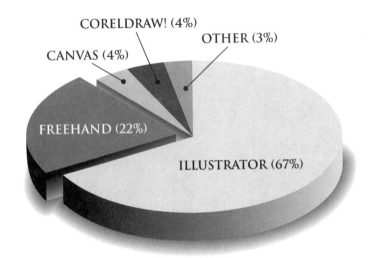

NOTE: THE INFORMATION REPRESENTED IN THIS GRAPH IS
NOT REAL, AND IS MEANT FOR ENTERTAINMENT PURPOSES ONLY

Creating a Graph

Illustrator has several different types of graphs you can use; *nine* to be exact: Column, Stacked Column, Bar, Stacked Bar, Line, Area, Scatter, Pie, and Radar (see Figure 19.2). Each of these types of graphs is used to present a different kind of data. If you aren't sure which type you need, don't worry; you can switch between graph types at any time, even after you've entered data.

Figure 19.2.

The many graph tools in Illustrator.

In Illustrator, you begin making a graph by defining the physical size of the graph. You do this in much the same way you draw a rectangle.

1. Select the desired Graph tool.
2. Press and drag to define a rectangle. (Holding down the (Option)[Alt] key while dragging draws out from the center.)

Alternatively, you can just click and Illustrator will prompt you with a dialog box where you can enter the dimensions of the graph numerically (see Figure 19.3).

19

Figure 19.3.

Entering graph dimensions numerically after clicking with the Graph tool.

The next step is giving Illustrator the facts—the actual values that will be used to make the graph actually mean something. After creating the bounding box for your graph, Illustrator presents you with the Graph Data dialog box (see Figure 19.4). If you've ever used Microsoft Excel or Lotus 1-2-3, this will look familiar to you.

Figure 19.4.

The Graph Data dialog box.

The next two icons are Revert and Apply. The Revert button sets the data in the graph back to the last saved version, whereas the Apply button lets you see your changes to the graph without closing the Graph Data dialog box. Closing the Graph Data dialog box applies the data to the graph.

Importing Graph Data

You can either enter data manually or import data from such programs as Excel or Lotus (or even from a tab-delimited text file). Notice that in the upper-right corner of the Graph Data dialog box are six icons. The left-most icon is the Import Data button. Click there to import data from an external file.

The next icon to the right is the Transpose button. This switches columns and rows of data, no matter what the graph type is.

Next is the Switch x/y button, which swaps the values of the *x* and *y* cells on a Scatter graph only.

Following the Switch x/y button is the Cell Style button. It is here where you can set the parameters for a selected cell (each box in the grid in the Graph Data window is a cell). You can set the number of decimals as well as the column width (see Figure 19.5). You can also change the column width manually by grabbing a vertical line and dragging it left or right (see Figure 19.6).

19

Figure 19.5.
The Cell Style dialog box.

Figure 19.6.
Adjusting the width of a column manually.

Editing Graph Data

What makes the graph function in Illustrator even more powerful is the ability to update the data in your graph. At any time, select the graph and choose Object➡Graphs➡Data. You are presented with the Graph Data dialog box again, where you can update the numbers. When you close the Graph Data dialog box, the graph is automatically updated with the new information.

Graph Options

After you create your graph, you can edit it to perfection. Choose Object➡Graphs➡Type and you are presented with the Graph Type dialog box. You are first presented with Graph Options (see Figure 19.7). Here you can change the type of graph, even though you selected another type earlier from the Toolbox. You can also choose where to place the Value Axis.

Figure 19.7.
The Graph Type dialog box.

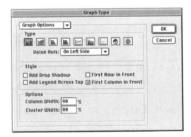

Besides options to add drop shadows or add a legend across the top, you can also set the column width and cluster width here (see Figure 19.8). These settings control the width and spacing of the bars or columns in a graph. Entering a number greater than 100% causes the columns to overlap and may produce very interesting effects (see Figure 19.9).

19

Figure 19.8.

Setting the column and cluster width.

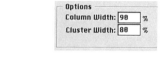

Figure 19.9.

Graphs set with different cluster widths.

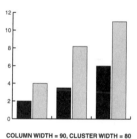

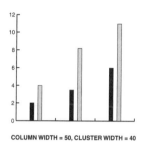

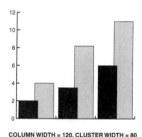

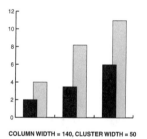

In the Graph Type dialog box, you can also specify settings for the Value Axis and Category Axis. Select them from the pop-up menu at the top of the dialog box (see Figure 19.10). In the Value Axis dialog box (see Figure 19.11), you can set the length of tick marks, which are the lines along the side of the graph that help indicate the position of data (see Figure 19.12). You can also specify the length of the tick marks (see Figure 19.13). Setting them at full length causes the tick marks to be drawn as lines throughout the entire graph. You can also specify these settings for the tick marks for the Category Axis (see Figure 19.14).

Figure 19.10.

Selecting Value Axis from the pop-up menu in the Graph Type dialog box.

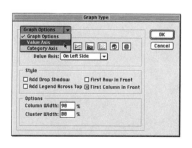

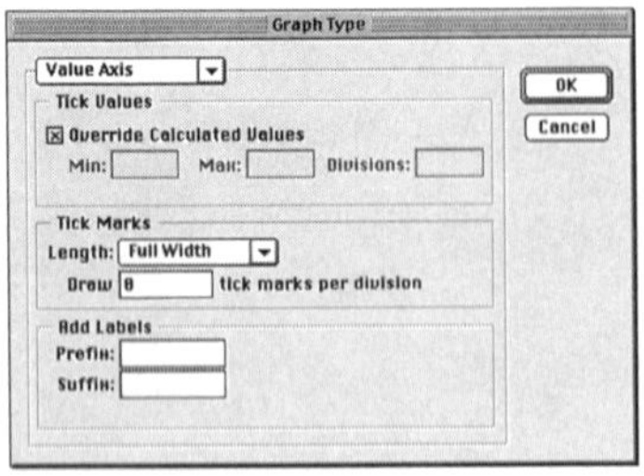

Figure 19.11.

The Value Axis dialog box.

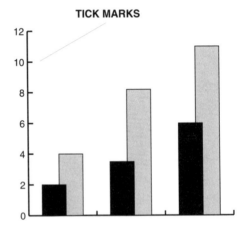

Figure 19.12.

Tick marks.

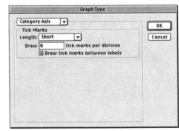

Figure 19.13.

Choosing tick mark specifications.

Figure 19.14.

The Category Axis dialog box.

19

Graph Design

Illustrator has a feature called Graph Design, which enables you to use any vector art to display information in your graphs. Say, for example, you are doing a report on how many shooting stars are seen each year. You would ordinarily make a bar graph, but to add a visual element to your graph, wouldn't it be great if you could use stars instead of boring bars? Here's how to do it:

1. First, we need to define the artwork for the bars. Draw a star, and then draw a square with a fill and stroke of none and send it behind the star (see Figure 19.15). In order to define a graph design, there must be a square behind your art to define the boundary of the art.

Figure 19.15.

Creating the star with a bounding box behind it.

2. With the art selected, choose Object➡Graphs➡Design.

3. Define the graph design by clicking New Design. Then click the Rename button to give your graph design a name. I called mine *star* (see Figure 19.16).

Figure 19.16.

Defining the graph design.

4. Now, let's create a graph. I used 350 and 560 for my data (see Figure 19.17).

Figure 19.17.

The "ordinary" graph.

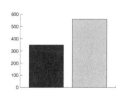

5. With the graph selected, choose Object➡Graphs➡Column.

6. In the Graph Column dialog box, select the star design and choose from the other options listed in the box. I chose a repeating column type so that the star appears for every 100 units, which I've also specified in the box. For fractions (350 and 560 do not represent full stars), I chose to have the stars chopped (see Figure 19.18); the other choice is to have them scaled.

Figure 19.18.

The Graph Column dialog box.

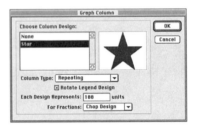

7. Click OK to see the newly designed graph (see Figure 19.19). Remember that you can always go back and tweak the design to get it just how you want it.

Figure 19.19.

The new graph in all its starry glory.

Ungrouping Your Graph

A graph is actually a group of many objects. You can ungroup a graph at any time, but be aware that when you do, the art loses its reference as a graph, and you are no longer able to make changes to it through the Graph Data and Graph Type dialog boxes. It's just like converting type into outlines: After you change it, you can no longer edit it as it was. Your best bet is to save a copy of the original graph before ungrouping so you can go back to it if needed.

Of course, after you ungroup the graph, you have complete and total freedom to do whatever you please with the graph elements. You can color them, run filters on them, and so on. Let your mind roam free, and you can create some really dynamic presentations.

19

Summary

Even though Illustrator is not known for its graphing capabilities, we just learned that Illustrator can really hold its own when it comes to creating great-looking charts. We learned how to import graph data from other applications, and we learned how to take that data and turn it into something that makes sense.

Term Review

Bounding box—The imaginary box surrounding a selected area.

Graph data—Numbers indicating relational information or data used to indicate a trend.

19

Hour **20**

Saving/Exporting Files

Without a doubt, the most important thing about a computer illustration is the ability to open it and edit it again and again. Compatibility with other software is important as well. You need to have the ability to bring your artwork into other applications, such as a page layout program. Illustrator does all of this, and more. With version 7, Illustrator is now completely cross platform, working identically in both Mac OS and Windows environments.

We all know how important it is to share, and this hour we focus on things such as:

☐ Saving Illustrator documents
☐ Exporting in PDF format
☐ Exporting in cross-platform formats

Saving in Illustrator Formats

When you save a file, you can choose between three different format options: Illustrator, Illustrator EPS, and Acrobat PDF. Each of these can be opened directly in any version of Illustrator and will retain the most information for future editing.

Native Illustrator

If your work will be done completely in Illustrator, then saving it in Illustrator format is best. The file will take up the smallest amount of disk space, it will open and save the fastest, and it will always be fully editable.

To save a file in Illustrator format, choose Save As from the File menu (see Figure 20.1). After giving your file a name and clicking the Save button, you are presented with a dialog box where you can specify what version of Illustrator you want your file saved in (see Figure 20.2). This is for compatibility purposes, and you should keep your file in Illustrator 7 format if possible.

JUST A MINUTE

Keeping your file in Illustrator 7 format ensures that any features specific to version 7 remain intact in your file. The capability to include URLs in an Illustrator file, for example, is only available in version 7. If you were to save your file in version 6 format, any URL information in your file would be lost (more on URLs in Illustrator in Hour 23, "Web Graphics").

Figure 20.1.

Choosing Save from the File menu.

Figure 20.2.

The Illustrator Format dialog box lets you ensure backwards compatibility with previous versions.

20

Illustrator EPS

If you need to open your file in other programs, then you want to use the Illustrator EPS format. *EPS* (Encapsulated PostScript) is a widely supported format. PostScript is a printer language created by Adobe that is built into many of today's printers and imagesetters. In order to print an EPS file, you must have a PostScript printer or a PostScript interpreter.

If you're not sure whether you have a PostScript printer, look for the Adobe PostScript logo (see Figure 20.3). Because PostScript must be licensed from Adobe, PostScript printers tend to be more expensive than those without PostScript. If you paid under $500 for your printer, it probably is not PostScript. You can use a PostScript interpreter, which is software that runs on your computer and that enables you to print PostScript files to a non-PostScript printer, but they tend to be very slow. Two such programs are *GCI StyleScript* and *Freedom of Press.*

Figure 20.3.

The Adobe PostScript logo.

Because an EPS file will be brought into other programs, you can choose to have a preview file embedded into the EPS. When you place the EPS into another program, the low-resolution preview enables you see how the file will look.

To save your file in Illustrator EPS format, choose Save As from the File menu and name your file. From the Format pop-up menu, choose Illustrator EPS and click the Save button. Illustrator then presents you with the EPS Format dialog box (see Figure 20.4). Here you can ensure compatibility with previous versions of Illustrator and choose to enclose placed images or fonts within the EPS file, as well as specify previews for viewing on either IBM PC or Macintosh.

Figure 20.4.

The EPS Format dialog box gives you control of file settings such as previews.

20

Acrobat PDF

The *PDF* format (Portable Document File) was developed by Adobe so that you can view documents, in their correct form, on any platform. Using the Adobe *Acrobat Reader*, you can view a PDF file on DOS, Macintosh, Windows, or UNIX. Because PDF uses PostScript technology as its base, you can open and edit a PDF file directly in Illustrator as well.

PDF files are good in several instances. If you're showing artwork to a client and they have a different system than you, all they need is Acrobat Reader to view it. PDF files can also be viewed on the World Wide Web with a Netscape Navigator plug-in called PDFViewer. Both Acrobat Reader and PDFViewer are free and available at http://www.adobe.com. PDF files can also be combined into multipage documents that can aid in making presentations.

To save your file in PDF format, choose Save As from the File menu and name your file. From the Format pop-up menu, choose Acrobat PDF, as shown in Figure 20.5, and click the Save button. If the PDF file will be viewed on a Windows or DOS machine, make sure you include the file extension of .PDF in the name (FILENAME.PDF).

Figure 20.5.

Choosing Acrobat PDF from the Format pop-up menu in the Save As dialog box.

Exporting to Other File Formats

As we mentioned earlier, Illustrator can export files in many different formats. Some are for placement in other illustration or paint programs, others are for high-end proprietary systems, and still others are for use on the World Wide Web. Some are vector formats, some are bitmap, and some, like EPS, can support both within the same file. Each format has its strengths and its weaknesses, which are discussed in this hour.

To export a file to any of these formats, choose Export from the File menu (see Figure 20.6) and choose a file format from the Format pop-up menu (see Figure 20.7).

Figure 20.6.

Choosing Export from the File menu.

Figure 20.7.

Choices from the Format pop-up menu in the Export dialog box.

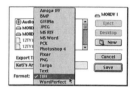

Based on what platform you have, all of the formats listed here may not be available to you. There are also file export formats that are available as plug-ins for Illustrator that are not listed here. Some are on the Illustrator CD, and others may be released on Adobe's web site (such as a FreeHand plug-in that enables you to open FreeHand documents in Illustrator).

TIFF

The *TIFF* format (Tag Image File Format) is a raster format that is supported both on the Macintosh platform and on the Windows platform. The TIFF format is widely supported and can be used in just about any page layout and paint program. Its format also has an option to use the LZW compression scheme, which makes for smaller file sizes without compromising detail.

When you choose to export your file as a TIFF, Illustrator presents you with the TIFF Options dialog box (see Figure 20.8). Here you can choose a resolution for your image as well as select a color model (RGB, CMYK, or Grayscale). If your image is intended to be viewed onscreen, select the Anti-Alias option to ensure there are no jaggy edges in your final image. You can also choose to include an ICC Profile (for color management) or LZW Compression. Finally, specify a byte order for the platform the file will be used on.

Figure 20.8.

The TIFF Options dialog box.

GIF89a, JPEG, PNG

The GIF89a, JPEG, and PNG formats are primarily used for files that will be viewed on the World Wide Web. All raster formats, these formats specialize in compressing information, which makes for small file sizes that can be transmitted quickly over modem phone connections. For more details on these formats, see Hour 23.

PCX

The PCX format is a bitmap that supports up to 24-bit color. It is primarily used on Windows machines and is actually the native format of PC Paintbrush—a paint program popular on

20

the Windows platform. Upon exporting a PCX file, Illustrator prompts you with a dialog box where you can specify what resolution the file should be (see Figure 20.9)

Figure 20.9.

The Resolution Options dialog box.

WMF

The Windows Metafile Format (WMF) is a vector file format for the Windows platform. It is supported by most Windows applications and does not require a PostScript printer to print. The quality of the image is questionable, though, and may not be desirable in all situations. It is best to run a test before using it on any particular image.

BMP means bitmap (literally—"bitmap image" means the same thing as "raster image") and is a standard format on Windows and DOS platforms. Besides prompting you to specify what resolution you want the image to be, Illustrator also prompts you with the BMP Options dialog box, where you can indicate Windows or OS/2 compatibility as well as bit depth and compression (see Figure 20.10).

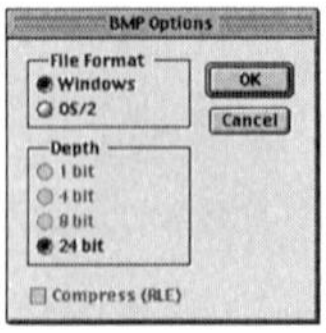

Figure 20.10.

The BMP Options dialog box.

Amiga IFF, TARGA, Pixar, PixelPaint

Amiga IFF, TGA (Targa), and Pixar are formats specific to proprietary graphics systems. PixelPaint is a Mac OS paint program. Whether it's 3D, animation, or full motion video, Illustrator has the capability to export to these programs, giving you the ability to create complex and exact elements in a comfortable environment before bringing them into high-end graphic systems for processing and enhancement.

20

Summary

Illustrator is not an island. We learned how important it is to be compatible and cross platform. We also learned about a whole lot of file formats and that each one has its strengths and weaknesses. Now we can use Illustrator together with other programs such as QuarkXPress and Photoshop, giving us unlimited creative capabilities in our quest for the ultimate design. You should be fairly comfortable with Illustrator by now as we begin the final stretch—just a few more hours. Hang in there! You're doing great!

Term Review

EPS — Encapsulated PostScript. A standard cross-platform image format based on the PostScript printer language. An EPS can contain vector images, pixel images, or both.

PDF — Portable Document File. Created by Adobe, this format was created to become a standard file format that could be viewed on any computer.

Acrobat Reader — The application necessary to view PDF files.

TIFF — Tagged Image File Format. A compression-capable format that is a standard on both Macs and PCs. A TIFF is a raster file.

20

Hour 21

Working Smart in Illustrator

We already know that there are several different ways to get any particular project done. To build a house, for example, you could use wood or bricks. Either way, you'll have a house, but one might be better than the other. The same applies to computer files—especially Illustrator documents. There might be several ways to "build" your document, but there is always a smart way, and a not-so-smart way. This chapter guides you in the right direction when creating your artwork in Illustrator. A great computer designer knows not only good design techniques but good production techniques as well, such as:

- ☐ Saving files
- ☐ Creating "clean" files
- ☐ Tracing images
- ☐ Managing placed images

Saving Your Files

If I told you that if you ate a large cheese pizza every day, you would live a long life, you would do it, right? And if I told you that by saving your files frequently, you can be assured that you will not lose data, you would do that too, right?

Saving your files is the most important part of working with computers. A computer will crash when you least expect it to (and it most certainly will crash when you expect it to), so save often. You might also want to use the Save As command to save documents as you create them, allowing you the luxury of quickly going back to any stage of your project as it was developed. You can name each file with version numbers, such as Pizza 1.1, Pizza 1.2, and so on, so you can quickly identify when each file was created.

Use Intelligent Filenames

Naming your file is more important than most people think. It's very important that you keep your files organized and that you name them so that you can quickly identify what each file is. On the Macintosh you were always able to create long filenames, and now you can in Windows 95, too. Take advantage of it. I remember when I used to name files "Bob's thingy" and "Logo with blue type." That's nice for being creative and all, but in two months when Bob needs his advertisement reprinted, you won't in a million years remember that you called it "thingy."

Also, if you're working in an environment with other designers and share your files with them, it's even more important to name your files so that other people can quickly identify and find them. If you have several versions of a logo, for example, you can name them like this: Apple Logo.B&W, Apple Logo.Process, and Apple Logo.Spot. Also, when you finish a job, you might even want to identify it like so: Apple Stationery.Final.

Working with Selections

Illustrator has a few tricks up its sleeve when it comes to making selections. Under the Edit menu there is a Select submenu that contains a few additional commands for making selections. Click an object, for example, and choose Select Same Fill. Illustrator then selects all objects in your document that have the same fill as the one you originally selected. The same applies for Select Same Stroke as well.

For even more selection tools, see Extensis VectorTools and ILLOM Toolkit in the "Using Third Party Plug-ins" section, later in this chapter.

21

Hiding and Locking

We learned that you can hide and lock artwork to make things easier when working on portions of your artwork, but this feature has one small problem. Although you can hide and lock items one at a time, you can only show or unlock all items at once. This means if you want to unlock just one item, you have to unlock everything, then select the items you want to remain locked, and lock them again.

To make things a bit easier, if you want to unlock just one item, unlock everything, then Shift-click the item you want to unlock and then select Object➡Lock again. This saves you the time of having to reselect everything again.

Keeping Your Documents Clean

You'll never find a mess on my computer. What you *will* find is an organized group of files. Even more importantly, each file in itself is "clean" and streamlined.

Allow me to explain. When you create a file, edit it, make revisions, and make revisions again, the file could contain many things that are not necessary in the final version. There may, for example, be times when you would leave some text loose in the document, such as notes for yourself or maybe a company's address. Or maybe you created a lot of guides. By deleting these after a file is complete, you are not only making the file smaller in size (saving precious disk space), but you are also creating a cleaner file that will print faster and have less of a chance of becoming corrupt.

Cleaning Up Individual Paths

Another important part of cleaning your files is deleting unnecessary anchor points. Many times, when you use the Autotrace tool (or even when importing files from Streamline), your Bézier paths contain extraneous anchor points. Of course, the more points there are in a document, the larger the file size, and the longer it takes to print.

Unfortunately, this is one thing in Illustrator that really needs some attention. Macromedia FreeHand has a simplify function that automatically removes points and smooths a selected path, and it would be a nice feature if Illustrator did this as well. Some people have FreeHand just for this purpose—they import the art into FreeHand to simplify it, and then bring it back into Illustrator to add the finishing touches.

One thing that Illustrator does have is a command called Cleanup (see Figure 21.1), which can be found by selecting Object➡Path➡Cleanup. This handy little janitorial function will gladly delete stray points (single anchor points with no paths), unpainted objects, and empty text paths. If only you had this when your mom told you to clean your room!

21

Figure 21.1.

The Cleanup dialog box.

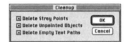

Scanning and Tracing Art

Not everything is created in Illustrator (although I'm sure Adobe would just *love* for that to happen), and many times we must scan logos and art sketches and then recreate them in Illustrator. True, there is the Autotrace tool, and even applications such as Streamline that were made to do this kind of thing, but more often than not, they produce less than desirable results. The best way to get logos and sketches into clean, good-looking vector art is to draw them from scratch yourself.

Relax, it's a lot easier than you might think. Illustrator has the tools to get you through. Let's take this one step at a time, shall we?

1. Scan your logo. You should scan your image at 72 dpi (we'll only be viewing it onscreen) and try to get it as large as possible without blowing out too much detail.

2. In Photoshop, or your favorite raster paint program, use the Levels feature to tint back or lighten your image so that it's only at 30 percent strength.

3. Save it in TIFF format. A TIFF does not use a preview for screen viewing but uses the actual file so that you get better detail when viewing it in Illustrator—especially when you zoom in close on it.

4. Open a new document in Illustrator.

5. Create a new layer and name it "template."

6. Place the scanned logo you just saved on the template layer and lock the layer (see Figure 21.2).

Figure 21.2.

Locking the template layer.

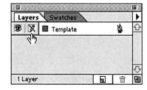

7. Create a new layer and name it "artwork."

8. We can now begin to trace the logo. The first step is to draw guides, which will help you as you recreate the logo (see Figure 21.3). Remember that you can turn any shape into a guide, so you can use circles or other shapes if necessary.

21

Figure 21.3.

Setting up guides to aid in tracing the logo.

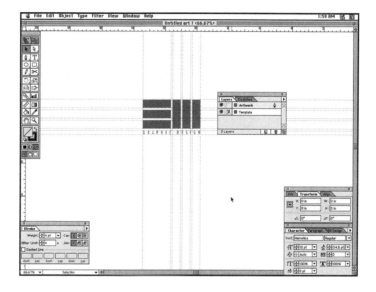

9. Next, try to see if you can recreate parts of the logo using simple shapes, the Rectangle and Ellipse tools, and the Pathfinder filters (see Figure 21.4).

Figure 21.4.

Using rectangles here greatly reduces the time to re-create the logo.

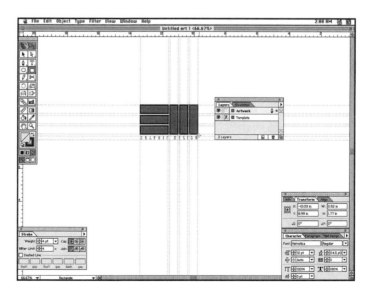

21

10. Finally, complete the rest of the logo using the Pen tool where necessary, and add any necessary fills and colors.

Using Third-party Plug-ins

Illustrator 7 has tremendous support for *plug-ins*—additions or extensions to Illustrator that add features, tools, and functionality. In fact, many parts of Illustrator are actually plug-ins themselves, such as the Layers palette. Adobe did this to make it easy to make modifications to the program and to keep Illustrator's core as clean as possible.

Of course, the most obvious advantage of the ability to have plug-ins is that other companies (or even ordinary people like yourself) can create plug-ins for Illustrator. Here I have listed plug-in packages from several vendors and have written short descriptions outlining their features.

Extensis VectorTools

Extensis VectorTools is probably the best collection of plug-ins on the market. A perfect mix of production-oriented and special effects plug-ins, VectorTools is a collection no serious illustrator should be without. VectorTools includes a magic wand selection tool for selecting multiple objects with similar attributes, and it also gives you the ability to edit colors using curves, just as in Photoshop. You can also turn 2D art into 3D art, set up object style sheets, and more!

Extensis Corporation
http://www.extensis.com

MetaCreations' KPT Vector Effects

KPT Vector Effects is part of the famous Kai's Power Tools suite of plug-ins and applications. Although its interface is just a tad different, KPT Vector Effects offers quick ways to create cool effects in Illustrator, including embossing, soft shadows, 3D, envelope distortion, and more.

MetaCreations
http://www.metacreations.com

HotDoor CADtools

CADtools is a great collection of over 34 drafting and dimensioning plug-ins. Even if you don't do drafting work, these plug-ins can really be useful. A good example is the Arc Tool, which enables you to draw arcs easily—a lot better than drawing whole circles and then deleting the parts you don't need.

Hot Door, Inc.
http://www.hotdoor.com

21

MAPublisher

If you are a cartographer or work a lot with maps, MAPublisher is for you. A suite of plug-ins, MAPublisher enables you to work with Geographic Information System (GIS) data directly in Illustrator. It also offers support for DXF files.

Avenza Software
http://www.avenza.com

Vertigo 3D Words

Vertigo is a company that makes 3D tools for use on powerful Silicon Graphics workstations. Recently, they began making plug-ins for use on Power Macintosh computers with Photoshop and Illustrator. 3D Words enables you to create true three-dimensional text and paths right in Illustrator.

Vertigo Software
http://www.vertigo3d.com

ILLOM Toolbox 1

Toolbox 1 is a wonderful collection of plug-ins that add some really great (and really cool) features to Illustrator. First of all, a Lasso tool lets you marquee select objects by drawing a path—just as in Photoshop. There's also search and replace for objects (so you can search for red stars and change them to yellow circles, for example) and text style sheets. Plug-ins for time tracking and enhanced transformations round out this excellent package.

ILLOM Development AB
http://www.illom.se

Preparing a File for Output

If you are sending your file out to a service bureau for film output or separations, you want to make sure that it prints right—the first time. Keeping your files clean, as mentioned earlier, is the first step in your quest for perfect film. Streamlining your files allows them to print faster (some service bureaus charge for processor time) and more reliably. Messy files have a tendency to crash or hang a RIP, the software that interprets files so they can be output on an imagesetter.

Include Typefaces and Linked Images

In order for anyone to print your file, they will need whatever typefaces you used as well as copies of any linked (placed) images. In many cases, you can avoid the typeface problem by converting your text to outlines. In fact, it's usually a good idea to convert your text to outlines whenever saving logos or mastheads that will be used repeatedly—you might forget about the typeface, thinking it's just a picture, when working in QuarkXPress or PageMaker.

21

To quickly check which fonts and linked images are in a particular file, choose Document Info from the File menu. Here Illustrator gives you an exhaustive list of your file's details and attributes, including linked and embedded images, as well as fonts used. You can save this information as a text file that you can then send to your service bureau. This might help them work on your file faster and more efficiently.

Convert Strokes to Paths

This is an important precaution. As you know, when scaling objects in Illustrator, you have the option to scale strokes as well as the rest of the object. If your art or logo has strokes of a specific weight, and then somebody scales the image without scaling the strokes, you might have a *slight* problem on your hands. By using the Convert Stroke to Path function, you eliminate the possibility of such a nightmare.

Blends and the Ink Pen Filter

There are two features in Illustrator that can really add a special touch to your document: blends and Ink Pen fills. These are also the two features in Illustrator that cause the most printing problems. Both the Blend tool and the Ink Pen filter create hundreds of objects to achieve their unique appearance, which can really tax even the latest RIPs. When using the Blend tool, you have an option to specify how many steps the blend should be. If you are creating a small blend that only covers a short distance, 40 objects may be sufficient, and very rarely will you need to create a blend with 255 objects (which is the default setting). As for the Ink Pen filter, use it on smaller objects if possible, or try to avoid using it excessively.

Working with Linked Images

We already know that you can place a raster image in Illustrator and have it linked to a file outside of your Illustrator document. If you've worked in QuarkXPress or PageMaker, you should already be familiar with this concept. You should also be familiar with the ability to update your linked images to reflect changes made to them after they're placed in an Illustrator file—a command missing from Illustrator. But fret not my dear friend; I'll tell you how to do it. There are two workarounds you can use to update linked images in Illustrator:

1. After you've updated and saved your raster image in your favorite raster application (such as Photoshop), return to your Illustrator document. Then, select the placed image you want to update. Choose Place from the File menu and choose the file you just updated. After clicking the Place button, Illustrator asks you if you want to replace the currently selected image. Choose Yes, and Illustrator replaces the old image with the updated one. Any transformations you had previously applied to that image such as scaling or rotating will be applied to the new image as well! (Note: This only works if the new image is still the same file format as before, such as TIFF or EPS.)

21

2. After you've updated your raster image in your favorite raster application (such as Photoshop), save it with the *exact same name*. Then return to Illustrator. Save and close your document, and then reopen it. Your images are then updated automatically.

Summary

This hour we learned a whole lot of tips and techniques on how to be more efficient when working with Illustrator files. We learned how important it is to save files with easily recognizable names, and we learned how clean files can save us a lot of aggravation. Plus we learned all about some really cool plug-ins available for Illustrator, as well as how to re-create scanned art. After this chapter, you have what it takes to add the title "production artist" to your business card.

Term Review

Plug-in—An extension or function that is added externally to the program.

RIP—Raster Image Processor. Software and/or hardware that bridges between a computer and an imagesetter.

Stray Point—A single anchor point that stands alone, with no path associated with it.

21

Hour 22

Printing

OK, you designed this beautiful piece of art, and now it's time to print it. Then you can show it to your mother who will be very proud of you and hang it on the refrigerator door (although she still doesn't know what exactly it is that you do).

Printing is an important part of the design process. If what you are designing will be used in print, it is a good idea to see how it looks on paper as opposed to onscreen. Sometimes it's difficult to visualize your art onscreen, and you can get a better grasp of it when viewed on paper. This is especially true with type. It might look okay at 12 point onscreen, but when you print it out on paper, you will realize that 11 or even 10 point would be much better. These subtle things often cannot be picked up onscreen. This chapter discusses:

- ☐ Printing your files
- ☐ Producing color separations
- ☐ The PostScript language
- ☐ Troubleshooting tips

Printing Files

One of the most basic functions of your computer is the Print command, and it works the same way in Illustrator as it would in just about any other program. To print a document, choose Print from the File menu (see Figure 22.1), or press (Command-P)[Control-P].

Figure 22.1.

Choosing Print from the File menu.

Document Setup/Page Setup

Way back in Hour 2, "Customizing Illustrator," we discussed the different settings in the Document Setup dialog box. There is also a Page Setup dialog box specific to your printer and print driver software. This dialog box is accessible through the Document Setup dialog box.

First, choose Document Setup from the File menu. Notice on the far right of the dialog box, under the Cancel button, is a button to open the Page Setup dialog box (see Figure 22.2). Your Page Setup dialog box contains settings for what paper tray to use and what orientation the page should print (portrait or landscape—tall or wide). Page Setup is Ilustrator's direct link to your printer, so the dialog box will be different based upon which printer drivers you are using (Laserwriter 7, Laserwriter 8, and so on), and the options available will also depend on what printer you are using.

Figure 22.2.

The Page Setup button in the Document Setup dialog box.

Tiling with the Page Tool

Not everything can fit on an 8 1/2×11 sheet of paper. When you have artwork that is larger than what your printer can handle, you can print the artwork in pieces and then paste the pieces together after the entire file has printed.

22

To indicate which part of your file gets printed, you use the Page Tool (H) (see Figure 22.3). Once the Page tool is selected, press and hold down the mouse button, and an outline appears (see Figure 22.4). Whatever is inside the borders of the outline will print. The artwork in your file is not affected in any way; you are simply instructing Illustrator as to which part of your document to print.

Figure 22.3.

The Page tool.

Figure 22.4.

Indicating which part of a document should print with the Page tool.

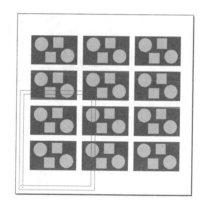

Color Separations

Before color artwork can actually be printed on press—be it CMYK, spot color, or Hexachrome (see note)—it must be separated. What that means is each color is printed on a separate page. If, for example, you are printing a four-color process job, you need to have four pages or *plates*—one each for cyan, magenta, yellow, and black. The process of making these plates is called *color separation* (see Figure 22.5).

JUST A MINUTE

Hexachrome was developed by Pantone to address one of the main shortcomings of CMYK printing: difficulty in printing bright and vibrant colors, specifically in the orange and green areas. By adding two more colors, Orange and Green, to CMYK, a much larger gamut (range of colors) is attainable. Essentially, this results in a 6-color job (CMYKOG), hence the name Hexachrome.

Figure 22.5.

A separated file.

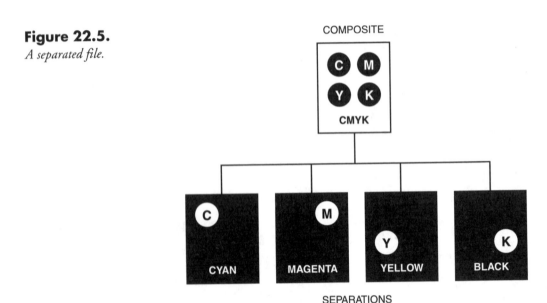

In most cases you send your files to a service bureau that prints the separations for you on film and provides you with a Matchprint (a high quality color proof, made directly from the film). But not every job needs to go to film, and there are times when printing separations on your laser printer are adequate. There are also times when I'll print separations to my laser printer to make sure they print correctly. Over the years, this has saved me thousands of dollars in potential film costs.

Printing Separations

If all of this talk about magenta and film is making you nervous, put down the book, take a deep breath, sip a beverage, and pick up the book again. Now let me tell you that printing separations is real easy in Illustrator. There are two ways to open Illustrator's Separation Setup dialog box.

☐ Choose Separation Setup from the File menu (see Figure 22.6).

☐ Click the Separation Setup button in the Print dialog box (see Figure 22.7).

After choosing one of these, you are presented with the Illustrator Separation dialog box (see Figure 22.8). Here you can specify how the separations should appear, as well as specify which colors should be separated, and how.

22

Figure 22.6.

Choosing Separation Setup from the File menu.

Figure 22.7.

Choosing Separation Setup from within the Print dialog box.

Figure 22.8.

The Separation dialog box.

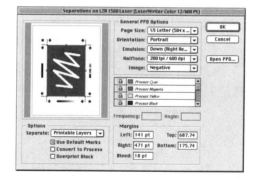

The first step you need to do is open a PPD file. A PostScript Printer Description file contains information about your printer such as resolution, available page sizes, and line screens.

Just a Minute

On a Macintosh your PPD files are located in a folder called Printer Descriptions. This folder can be found in the Extensions folder in your System Folder.

In Windows, your PPD files are located in the Windows subdirectory.

To specify a PPD file, click the Open PPD button (see Figure 22.9), navigate to where your PPD files are and click the Open button.

Figure 22.9.
The Open PPD button.

After a PPD file is loaded, you can specify options for your separations such as Page Size, Orientation, Emulsion, Halftone, and Image (see Figure 22.10). If you don't know what specifications you should use, consult your printer or production expert.

Figure 22.10.
General PPD options.

Specifying Colors to be Separated

This is the most important part of separating a file: Choosing which inks will print, and how they will separate. In the center of the Separations dialog box is a list of colors that are used in your document. A printer icon in the box to the left of a color indicates that the color will print to its own plate (see Figure 22.11).

Figure 22.11.
In this example, magenta and black print, but the yellow plate does not.

To print spot colors, uncheck the Convert to Process checkbox (see Figure 22.12). Otherwise, spot colors are converted to process and separated as a process color, as indicated by a process color icon (see Figure 22.13).

Figure 22.12.
The Convert to Process checkbox, located in the lower-left corner of the Separation dialog box.

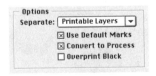

22

Figure 22.13.
*In this example, the icon
indicates the spot color
brown will be converted
and will print as a
process color.*

Positioning the Plate

You can also position the separation on the page by grabbing the edge and moving it as shown
in Figure 22.14.

Figure 22.14.
*Positioning the artwork
on the page by grabbing
the cropmarks and
dragging.*

Setting Cropmarks

Cropmarks are very important. They indicate to the printer where to trim the paper around
your artwork. If your artwork contains bleeds (where the artwork goes past the edge of the
paper), then crop marks are the only indication as to where the page should end. Follow these
steps to create accurate cropmarks:

1. Draw a rectangle that exactly matches your trim size.

2. Position your artwork within the rectangle (or position the rectangle over the
   artwork).

3, Choose Make Cropmarks from the Object menu (see Figure 22.15)

Figure 22.15.
Making cropmarks.

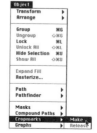

You cannot move or edit cropmarks after you make them unless you select Release Cropmarks from the Object menu. If you do not have a rectangle selected when you choose Make Cropmarks, Illustrator draws cropmarks based on the page size.

JUST A MINUTE

> You'll remember that back in Hour 17, "Vector Filters," we learned about a filter called Create Trim Marks. Trim marks (Filter➡Create➡Trim Marks), however, and Cropmarks (Object➡Make➡Cropmarks) are different. Trim marks are simply lines that Illustrator draws for you. They are editable in that you can color them, change their thickness, and even delete individual lines. Cropmarks on the other hand are non-editable, and you can only have one set of Cropmarks in a single document.

PostScript

At the heart of Illustrator is the PostScript printing language. Developed by Adobe, PostScript is probably responsible for the success of the desktop publishing industry as well as the use of computers for graphic design services.

In order to take advantage of Illustrator's capabilities, you must use a PostScript printer. If a printer does not have PostScript, or a PostScript interpreter, you will get undesirable results, such as noticeable jaggy edges and the printed colors may not match what you see onscreen.

Troubleshooting

Although we hope it never happens, there are times when a file fails to print due to an error. Many times it is because the document is too complex for the printer it is being printed on, or there is a software incompatibility. If such an event occurs, try the following tips:

- ☐ Use the Split Long Paths option, which we discussed back in Hour 2. This option can be found in General Preferences.
- ☐ Use the Compatible Gradient Printing option, which we discussed in Hour 2. This option can also be found in General Preferences.
- ☐ Do a Save As on the file in an earlier Illustrator format. Illustrator 7 utilizes PostScript 3.0 commands (see the previous section on PostScript), which may confuse some older printers. Saving in an older format, such as Illustrator 6, may help.

☐ Isolate the culprit. Delete parts of your illustration one by one, starting with placed images first, sending your file to the printer until it prints. Sometimes a file may become corrupt or a particular shape may be causing a problem.

☐ Copy and paste your illustration into a new file. Sometimes a file may become corrupt, and the best way to correct it is to destroy it.

22

Summary

Things started out real easy as we learned to print our Illustrator documents. Things got a bit harder when we learned all about color separations and trapping issues. As if that weren't enough, we finished with a flair as we learned a bit about the PostScript printing language.

Well, I had a lot of fun, and I hope you did, too, as you learned all about Illustrator. Because the computer field is ever-changing, visit my web site at http://www.mordy.com for the latest information on Illustrator. And don't forget to send me email at mordy@mordy.com.

Term Review

PostScript—A programming language developed by Adobe Systems for printing and page layout purposes.

Separations—The process of preparing individual color plates for printing.

Tiling—Splitting up a large page into smaller parts for printing purposes.

Cropmarks—Marks or lines that indicate to a printer where to cut the paper.

Hexachrome—A six-color printing process developed by Pantone, Inc.

Hour 23

Web Graphics

At first everyone thought it was just a fad, but recently the Internet—or more specifically, the World Wide Web—has become a part of our daily lives. Email addresses and URLs are exchanged as often as street addresses and phone numbers. Although the Internet has been around for quite some time, the World Wide Web turned the Internet into what it is today because of two essential features: images and links. Illustrator brings the power of these two features into the palm of your hand. This hour, we cover topics such as:

☐ Web-safe color issues

☐ Assigning URLs to objects

☐ Exporting in web-compatible formats

☐ Animation

Designing for the Web

I mentioned earlier that the web offers two powerful features: images and links. As the old saying goes, a picture is worth a thousand words, and using images to convey your message can be very effective. You can easily create images in Illustrator for use on the web (see Figure 23.1).

Figure 23.1.
*Creating eye-catching
illustrations for the web
is easy in Illustrator.*

A link is something on a Web page that, when you click it, takes you to another page. A link can be specified in your HTML document as either text or a picture (see the following Just a Minute). A picture can also have multiple links, meaning you can specify different links for different parts of your image (see Figure 23.2). This is called an *imagemap*. Illustrator can create web-ready graphics, but before we begin making our art, we need to know a few things about the web.

Figure 23.2.
*By defining an
imagemap, you can
specify a different link
setting for each button in
this image.*

JUST A MINUTE

HTML documents are created in a text editor or an HTML editor application. HTML, Hypertext Markup Language, is the standard programming language used on the World Wide Web. If you're squeamish and don't want to get involved in "writing code," there are plenty of WYSIWYG (What You See Is What You Get) HTML editors out there, such as Adobe PageMill and Claris HomePage, that do all the programming for you.

Color on the Web

When you design a brochure that will be printed, you have control over how the final product appears. You specify exact colors and papers to give a precise look and feel to the brochure. On the web, however, you have very little control as to how your art appears to the different people who view it. Some people might have a small, cheap monitor that displays only 256 colors. Other people may have large high-resolution monitors set to millions of colors. And if that weren't enough, different browsers such as Netscape Navigator and Microsoft Internet Explorer have different settings, so what looks perfect on your screen may look completely different on someone else's.

23

Dithered Colors

When you create an image on a computer with millions of colors, what happens when you view that image on a computer that only has 256 colors? Well, the results can be horrifying at times. If a computer does not have a certain color in its palette, it tries to approximate the color by arranging a variety of pixels in the same vicinity to give the appearance of that color. This process is called dithering. Sometimes the dithering is presentable, but usually it creates odd and distracting patterns and can also make text unreadable (see Just a Minute).

JUST A MINUTE

Dithering is a lot like screening in traditional printing. When the screens are rotated just right, you get a nice rosette, but if the screens do not line up properly, you get an ugly moiré pattern.

23

Using the Web Palette

As Douglas Adams would say, "Don't Panic." There are a few things you can do to assure that your art looks great on the web—on any machine. The first thing is to use the Web-safe color palette. As we learned in Hour 9, "Coloring Objects," computer monitors use the RGB color model. The web-safe color palette is a collection of 216 RGB colors that will not dither when viewed onscreen.

How did they come up with a number such as 216? Well, it's like this: The majority of people out there have monitors with 256 colors (VGA is 256 colors). These 256 colors are in what's called the system palette, which is built into your operating system. The Windows system palette and the Macintosh system palette, however, differ slightly. To be exact, there are 40 colors that do not match up between the two system palettes. So, if we eliminate those 40 colors, we are left with 216 colors that are identical on both platforms (see the following Just a Minute).

JUST A MINUTE

If you are creating artwork for an intranet, where you know the type of computers people are using, you can take advantage of that by using more resources. If, for example, everyone who will be viewing your art has a Macintosh, you can use the Macintosh system palette that contains 40 more colors than the web palette does.

Now, if we would create artwork using only colors from these palettes, we can be sure that the colors will not dither when viewed on the web. By now, you're wondering, "Great! Where do I sign up?" and the answer is easy. Adobe has included system palettes for both Windows and Macintosh as well as a color-safe web palette—all right inside Illustrator. Simply choose

Swatch Libraries from the Window menu and make your choice (see Figure 23.3). The Palette opens in a new Swatches-like floating palette and is not editable (see Figure 23.4). If you want to edit colors, you must drag those colors to the Swatches palette first, and then edit them.

Figure 23.3.

Opening the web palette.

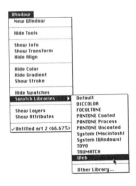

Figure 23.4.

The Web palette looks and acts similar to the Swatches palette. Notice the little icon in the lower-left corner, indicating the palette cannot be edited.

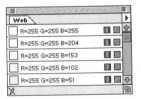

JUST A MINUTE

Because the web and the technology that it brings are constantly changing, dealing with every aspect of web color can take up an entire book in itself. Although many issues and techniques are beyond the scope of this book, you might want to look into books that delve deeper into web color, such as *The PANTONE Web Color Resource Kit* or *Creating Killer Web Sites*, both published by Hayden Books.

Assigning URLs to Objects

We mentioned before that a single image, otherwise known as an imagemap, can contain multiple links. Using an imagemap allows a user to follow different links, based on where he clicks in a linked image. Before Illustrator 7, you had to create an imagemap in a third-party application, which was usually a tedious task. And if you made a change to your image, you would have to redefine the imagemap as well. Now, with Illustrator 7, you can do it all in one application, and in one easy step.

23

You create an imagemap by assigning a URL (Uniform Resource Locator) to an object in your illustration. URL is a fancy word used for a web address, and usually looks similar to this: http://www.adobe.com. In order for you to create an imagemap, you must know the URL of the page you are linking to.

To assign a URL to an object, open the Attributes palette (F11). Select an object, and type the correct URL in the Attributes palette (see Figure 23.5). After you enter a URL, it is added to the pop-up list in the Attributes palette, so you can choose from a list as you create more links (see Figure 23.6).

Figure 23.5.

Entering a URL in the Attributes palette.

Figure 23.6.

Choosing a link from the pop-up menu in the Attributes palette.

If you have a web browser such as Netscape Navigator or Microsoft Internet Explorer, and an Internet connection, you can click the Launch Browser button in the Attributes palette to check your links.

Web File Formats

You must save your file in a certain file format before it can be used for the World Wide Web. The most popular formats, GIF and JPEG, can be saved right out of Illustrator, and each has its strengths and weaknesses. Another file format, PNG, is slowly making its way into the limelight as well because it offers some features not found in GIF or JPEG. Basically, all of these formats use a compression method to make the files smaller so that they take less time to transfer over a modem.

All files saved in these formats are converted to pixels when they are saved. Always be sure to keep a copy of your original Illustrator files in case you need to make changes to your images. Also, be careful when you save your web files that you give appropriate names to your images. Use only lowercase letters, no spaces, and use the appropriate three-letter extension for your file (GIF, JPG, PNG) so that a browser can identify it.

The GIF89a Format

The GIF89a format (created in 1989, hence the 89a extension) is probably the most popular file format used for images on the web. Developed by the people at CompuServe, GIF uses a lossless compression scheme called LZW. Lossless means that no information is lost when the file is compressed. The GIF format is best used for images with flat color, such as logos and illustrations.

Exporting a GIF

1. Choose Export from the File menu (see Figure 23.7).

Figure 23.7.

Choosing the Export command.

2. Choose GIF89a from the pop-up menu (see Figure 23.8).

Figure 23.8.

Choosing the GIF89a file format.

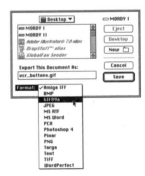

3. Give your file a name (don't forget the .GIF extension) and click the Save button.
4. Choose your options from the GIF89a Options dialog box and click OK (see Figure 23.9).

23

Figure 23.9.

The GIF89a Options dialog box.

Let's take a closer look at some of the options presented in the GIF89a Options dialog box. First, you can select a palette of colors to be saved with the file (see Figure 23.10). Choose either the Web palette or the Adaptive palette to get even fewer colors. The GIF format supports any number of colors up to 256. The fewer colors in the palette, the smaller your file size. You then have four options: Interlace, Transparent, Anti-alias, and Imagemap.

Figure 23.10.

Choosing from different palette options.

Selecting the Interlace option enables your image to appear gradually onscreen when it appears in a browser window. This gives the viewer an idea of what the image looks like as it loads.

Using Transparent makes the background of your image appear as if it were filled with nothing, letting colors that appear behind it show through. This is important with irregularly shaped or oval images, which would otherwise appear with a white background.

Anti-alias, as we mentioned earlier with the Rasterize command, smoothes out jaggy lines and curves, making the image look better onscreen. Try to avoid using this option with small font sizes as it tends to make the type too blurry to read.

Finally, if you have assigned URLs in your file, you can export an imagemap along with the GIF file. You can choose to create either a client-side imagemap or a server-side imagemap. Client-side imagemaps are generally better and are more common in today's web sites.

The JPEG Format

The JPEG format (pronounced jay-peg) uses a lossy compression scheme, meaning that information is thrown out in order to make the file size smaller. This affects the final quality of the image, and you are able to specify how much information is lost during compression (of course, the more you throw out, the smaller the file becomes). JPEG is used primarily for photographic images or complex illustrations with gradients because the JPEG format can support 24-bit color (millions of colors).

Exporting a JPEG

1. Choose Export from the File menu.
2. Choose JPEG from the Format pop-up menu (see Figure 23.11).

Figure 23.11.

Choosing JPEG from the Format pop-up menu.

3. Give your file a name (don't forget the .JPG extension) and click Save.
4. Choose your options from the JPEG Options dialog box and press OK (see Figure 23.12).

Figure 23.12.

The JPEG Options dialog box.

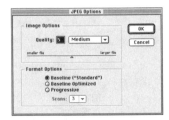

In the JPEG Options dialog box, you are able to set the image quality, which also controls the amount of compression (see Figure 23.13). By selecting a higher quality file, you are also creating a larger file. To change the quality, simply drag the little triangle slider to the left or right or enter a number from 1–10 in the box.

23

Figure 23.13.

Setting the image quality.

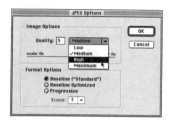

Recently, a new kind of JPEG format, called progressive JPEG, has begun to spread and is supported by the latest versions of popular web browsers. A progressive JPEG is essentially the same as an interlaced GIF, where the file loads gradually, enabling the viewer to get an idea of what the image is as it loads. I have even found that progressive JPEGs are usually a few K smaller than a Baseline (standard) JPEG.

The PNG Format

The PNG format (pronounced "ping") was initially created to address the shortcomings of the GIF format. Using a completely new compression algorithm, it avoids any legal problems concerning the LZW compression scheme (see the following Just a Minute). PNG also supports 24-bit color, as well as the use of alpha channels for masking. The format, however, is new on the scene, and is supported in very few browsers.

JUST A MINUTE

The GIF format utilizes the LZW compression scheme that was developed by Unisys Corporation. A few years ago, after a long legal battle, Unisys began to charge software developers a royalty fee if they created software that implemented the LZW compression algorithm (end users are not charged, only developers). The PNG format was developed as an alternative to the GIF format, to avoid having to pay royalty fees to Unisys.

Exporting a PNG

1. Choose Export from the File menu.
2. Choose PNG from the Format pop-up menu (see Figure 23.14).

Figure 23.14.

Choosing PNG from the Format pop-up menu.

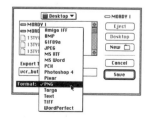

3. Give your file a name (don't forget the .PNG extension) and click Save.

4. Choose a resolution from the Resolution Options dialog box and press OK (see Figure 23.15). Because your art will be viewed on the web, 72 dpi is fine.

Figure 23.15.

The Resolution Options dialog box.

5. Choose your options from the PNG Options dialog box and press OK (see Figure 23.16).

Figure 23.16.

The PNG Options dialog box.

PNG's interlacing scheme is called Adam7, or you can choose to have no interlacing. You can also choose from several filters, which are different compression methods. The Adaptive method is most effective for web images.

Making Animations

Illustrator's Blend tool can help you create great-looking animations for the web. The GIF89a file format supports multiple images in a single file, enabling animation. Almost all of today's web browsers support GIF89a animation.

Basically, an animation is a string of images or frames, where each frame is different than the next. When viewed one after the other, the image appears to move. You can use Illustrator's Blend tool to help create the different frames.

1. Create two objects—one is the object in its original state, the other in the state you eventually want it to be (see Figure 23.17).

Figure 23.17.

Two different objects.

2. Select both objects.

3. Choose the Blend tool (B) from the Toolbox (see Figure 23.18).

Figure 23.18.
Illustrator's Blend tool.

4. Click one point from the first object (see Figure 23.19).

Figure 23.19.
Selecting the point to blend from.

5. Click a corresponding point on the second object (see Figure 23.20).

Figure 23.20.
Selecting the point to blend to.

6. Specify the number of steps Illustrator should create (this is the number of frames).

You can then tweak each object individually (see Figure 23.21). In order to create the actual animation file, you need to export each frame as a separate GIF file, and then combine them in a third-party animation program such as GifBuilder (for Mac OS) or GIF Construction Set (for Windows).

Figure 23.21.
After the blend is performed (top), you can tweak and edit each object (bottom).

The Blend tool can also be used to create airbrush effects by creating more steps. Experiment with blending small, light-colored objects within larger, dark-colored objects to create highlights and shadows. Keep in mind that blends can create a lot of shapes that make for slower print times and larger file sizes. For more information on using the Blend tool, see Hour 21, "Working Smart in Illustrator."

Summary

This hour you became a techie web-head! We learned all about using "safe" colors when designing for the web to prevent dithering. We also learned how to create imagemaps by assigning URLs to objects right in Illustrator. And if that weren't technical enough, we learned how to make our images web-ready by saving them in a variety of web-compatible formats. Heck, we even covered animation!

We're getting ready to wrap things up next hour when we learn how to print stuff and make color separations, so get ready for the home stretch!

Term Review

Imagemap—A list of coordinates that, when referenced to a graphic image, enable the user to follow different links, depending on where they click on the image.

Interlacing—The process of loading an image gradually, increasing in resolution and detail as it appears in the browser.

Adaptive Color Palette—A table of a specific number of colors that are derived from the best possible match in an image.

Web Color Palette—A table of 216 specific colors that can be reliably used in any browser and on any platform.

GIF, JPEG, PNG—Image file formats that are universally accepted on the Internet and World Wide Web.

23

Hour 24

Cross-Platform Issues

As we begin the last chapter of this book, it's important to remember that the beauty of working with a computer is that anything that you create can be worked on not only on your machine but others as well. Whether it be a co-worker, a client, a service bureau, or even just moving files between your office and computer at home, it's a good idea that you become familiar with moving your files around. As we mentioned before, Illustrator is cross-platform. This means the program works the same way on both Macintosh and Windows computers, and, more importantly, it means you can open the same file on either platform as well.

This sounds really nice on paper, but it's important to remember that it doesn't always work like that in real life. There are several important issues that you should keep in mind when working with files that will be used on both Macintosh and Windows platforms. Throughout the next hour, we explore these issues, including:

- [ ] Naming files
- [ ] Fonts
- [ ] Drag and drop
- [ ] Color management

Naming and Saving Files

Be careful when naming your files. The Mac OS supports filenames of up to 32 characters, as does Windows 95, but Windows 3.1 and DOS support only 12 characters in the form "XXXXXXXX.XXX."

If you are saving a file on a Macintosh for use on a PC, name the file with the appropriate *file extension* preceded by a period (.EPS, .TIF, .GIF, .JPG, and so on). If your file will be opened in Illustrator for Windows, save it with the Illustrator extension ("FILENAME.AI"), or Illustrator will not open the file. (Although Macintosh can tell the kind of file from the file resource type, Windows relies on the three-letter extension to identify the file type.)

If you are copying your file onto a disk or a removable media cartridge, such as a zip disk, be sure the disk is formatted for the computer it will be used on. Although support for PC disks is built-in to the Mac OS, you need a special utility to mount Macintosh disks on a Windows machine.

Patterns and Gradients

Expand your gradients and patterns where possible (we learned how to do this using the Expand command in Hour 10, "Fills"). This is just a precaution you can take to ensure the integrity of your gradients or patterns in a file. This is especially important when transferring files to a computer that uses an older version of Illustrator than what you are currently using. Patterns and Gradients as we know them now did not exist in versions prior to version 5 on the Macintosh and 4.1 on Windows.

Drag and Drop

Drag and drop is a feature in today's operating systems that greatly increases productivity. Instead of having to copy and paste something from one application to another, you can simply drag your selection right into another application window. If, for example, you are working in Illustrator, and want to bring some artwork into Photoshop, you can simply drag the object from the Illustrator window right into the Photoshop window.

Of course, in order to take advantage of these drag and drop features, you must have enough RAM in your computer to run both Illustrator and Photoshop simultaneously (or any other programs that you want to drag objects into or from).

You can drag a bitmap image from Photoshop 4 into Illustrator, but it will be converted to a 72 dpi RGB image regardless of what the settings were for that file in Photoshop.

24

When dragging selected Illustrator objects into Photoshop 4, you can hold down the Shift key to place the object in the center of the active layer, and you can also hold down the (Command)[Control] key to have the Illustrator art placed as paths in Photoshop (for use as clipping paths and selections).

You can also drag objects directly to your desktop. On a Macintosh this creates a clipping file (PICT), and in Windows this creates a scrap file (WMF).

Font Issues

There are two leading font technologies out in the world of publishing: TrueType and Postscript Type 1. TrueType was developed by both Apple and Microsoft, and PostScript Type 1 was developed by Adobe. A few years ago, there was a showcase showdown between these two technologies, and when the dust settled PostScript remained the standard on the Macintosh platform, but TrueType became the de facto on the Windows side.

This can make for some problems when switching documents between platforms—especially in documents with kerning or justification. Whenever possible, it's best to convert your text to outlines to avoid any problems. Of course, if the type must be edited, then converting the type to outlines won't work for you. Just be prepared to see different line breaks and letter spacing when moving the file between platforms.

To ensure that fonts appear identical across platforms, make sure the font names are identical and that they are from the same type foundry (Adobe Garamond is very different from ITC Garamond).

Compatibility

Cross-platform compatibility in Illustrator 7 is greatly improved from previous versions. Illustrator now supports many different file formats. Of course, whenever possible, try to keep your file in EPS format as this keeps the file in a scalable format, as well as ensures that your file prints reliably from any PostScript printer.

Color Management

We spoke about color management back in Hour 16, "Working with Raster Images," but I thought it was necessary to repeat it again. In all probability, what you see on a Macintosh screen will vary greatly from what you see on a Windows screen. If possible, try to use standard defined colors, such as those from the PANTONE collection, and use a printed swatchbook to proof colors.

24

Summary

In order to be successful in today's growing world of computer design, one must be able to work with both platforms. We already knew that Illustrator was a cross-platform application, but this past hour we learned all about the little things—the things that matter most—to help ensure a smooth transition between both Macintosh and Windows platforms.

Term Review

Drag and drop—Copying items between applications or open windows by simply dragging the selected items without using Copy and Paste commands.

File extension—Following the period in a filename, up to three letters that identify the file type, such as EPS or TIF. (Applies to PC only. Mac OS uses a file resource located within the file to determine the file type.)

24

INDEX

Other DESIGN/GRAPHICS Titles

Photoshop 4 Studio Skills

Photoshop 4 Studio Skills is the fast, fun, easy way to learn the features of this powerful graphics program.

- Explore the ins and outs of the newest features of Photoshop 4
- Find out how to create Photoshop images for the web
- Learn how to effectively work in layers and grayscale
- Discover the best methods for working with color

Steven Moniz
1-56830-356-4 ■ $35.00 USA/$49.95 CDN
352 pp., 7 3/8 x 9 1/8, Covers PC and Macintosh
Available Now

Adobe FAQ
1-56830-372-6 ■ $50.00 USA/$71.00 CDN
Available Now

Photoshop Textures Magic
1-56830-368-8 ■ $39.99 USA/$56.95 CDN
Available Now

Classroom in a Book: Adobe Illustrator
1-56830-371-8 ■ $45.00 USA/$63.95 CDN
Available Now

Classroom in a Book: Adobe PageMaker
1-56830-370-x ■ $45.00 USA/$61.95 CDN
Available Now

Classroom in a Book: Adobe Photoshop
1-56830-317-3 ■ $45.00 USA/$63.95 CDN
Available Now

Illustrator Type Magic
1-56830-334-3 ■ $39.99 USA/$56.95 CDN
Available Now

Photoshop Magic: Expert Edition
1-56830-416-1 ■ $55.00 USA/$77.95 CDN
Available November 1997

Illustrator 7 Complete
1-56830-364-5 ■ $45.00 USA/$63.95 CDN
Available Now

Digital Type Design Guide
1-56830-190-1 ■ $45.00 USA/$61.95 CDN
Available Now

Digital Prepress Complete
1-56830-328-9 ■ $55.00 USA/$77.95 CDN
Available Now

Photoshop Type Magic
1-56830-220-7 ■ $35.00 USA/$47.95 CDN
Available Now

Photoshop Type Magic 2
1-56830-329-7 ■ $39.99 USA/$56.95 CDN
Available Now

Photoshop 4 Complete
1-56830-323-8 ■ $45.00 USA/$61.95 CDN
Available Now

PageMaker 6.5 Complete
1-56830-331-9 ■ $45.00 USA/$61.95 CDN
Available Now

Stop Stealing Sheep & find out how type works
0-672-48543-5 ■ $19.95 USA/$26.99 CDN
Available Now

Visit your fine local bookstore, or for more information visit us at http://www.hayden.com

Other GRAPHICS/3D & MUTLIMEDIA Titles

DeBabelizer: The Authorized Edition

Learn how to optimize images for creative work with DeBabelizer...the essential tool for anyone working with computer graphics. This book is a must for creative professionals specializing in graphic design, Web design, multimedia or game creation. Easy-to-follow, this comprehensive guide offers techniques for using DeBabelizer to produce sharp, high-quality graphic images.

- CD-ROM contains the Lite version of DeBabelizer as well as Photoshop plug-ins and sample graphic images
- Provides extensive visual examples to illustatrate key production techniques in all areas of graphics processing
- Offers techniques for using SuperPalette to optimize images

Jason Yeaman & Mark Barnes
1-56830-324-6 ■ $45.00 USA/$63.95 CDN

192 pp., 7 3/8 x 9 1/8, Covers Version 2.1 for Windows, Macintosh, and UNIX, Accomplished - Expert
Available Now

Workflow Reengineering
1-56830-265-7 ■ $30.00 USA/$40.95 CDN
Available Now

Creating Your Digital Portfolio—A Guide to Marketing and Self Promotion
1-56830-326-2 ■ $34.99 USA/$49.95 CDN
Available Now

FreeHand Graphics Studio Skills
1-56830-302-5 ■ $45.00 USA/$63.95 CDN
Available Now

Imaging Essentials
1-56830-051-4 ■ $39.95 USA/$53.99 CDN
Available Now

Infini-D Revealed
1-56830-222-3 ■ $45.00 USA/$61.95 CDN
Available Now

Kai's Magic Toolbox
1-56830-223-1 ■ $45.00 USA/$61.95 CDN
Available Now

Live Picture Revealed
1-56830-263-0 ■ $45.00 USA/$61.95 CDN
Available Now

Adobe Premiere for Windows: Classroom in a Book, Second Edition
1-56830-172-3 ■ $50.00 USA/$68.95 CDN
Available Now

Macromedia Director Lingo Workshop for Windows
1-56830-269-X ■ $45.00 USA/$63.95 CDN
Available Now

Interactivity by Design
1-56830-221-5 ■ $40.00 USA/$54.95 CDN
Available Now

Photoshop Type Magic 2
1-56830-329-7 ■ $39.99 USA/$56.95 CDN
Available Now

Still Images in Multimedia
1-56830-273-8 ■ $45.00 USA/$63.95 CDN
Available Now